The Irish Language
in
NORTHERN IRELAND

Edited by
Aodán Mac Póilin

THE IRISH LANGUAGE IN NORTHERN IRELAND

Cóipcheart/Copyright © Aodán Mac Póilin 1997 (*eagarthóir*/editor)

Is leis na húdair cóipcheart a n-aistí féin
Copyright for each essay resides with the individual author

ISBN: 0–9516466–3-x
The Irish Language in Northern Ireland

Clúdach/Binding: *clúdach bog*/paperback.

Arna fhoilsiú ag/Published by:
Iontaobhas ULTACH / ULTACH Trust
Seomra 202, Teach an Fhuaráin, 19 Plás Dhún na nGall, Béal Feirste, BT1 5AB
Room 202, Fountain House, 19 Donegall Place, Belfast, BT1 5AB

Gach ceart ar cosnamh/All rights reserved

Cló agus Ceangal/Printed and bound by:
GPS Colour Graphics Limited, Belfast

Foreword

The essays here are designed to stimulate constructive debate on the Irish language in Northern Ireland. In a society where communication takes the form of cliches being hurled back and forth across no-man's-land, it is not always easy for Irish language enthusiasts to find the space for a reasonable discussion. This book represents an attempt to create such a space.

The essays draw on a number of disciplines; history, anthropology, sociolinguistics, and four of them are based on doctoral research. The authors were asked to make their work as accessible as possible to the general reader, and to cut down on learned gobbledygook.

Inevitably, some themes recur throughout the book. The relationship between political ideology and the language movement is discussed in all the essays, and a number of contributers offer varying interpretations of the role of Douglas Hyde. No attempt was made to impose order on such overlapping themes: in itself, the variety of opinion expressed here both reflects and contributes to the debate within the language movement.

Much remains to be covered: *Comhaltas Uladh*, Irish-medium education and Irish in English-medium schools, the residual Gaeltachts within Northern Ireland in the early days of the state, the relationship of the Catholic church with the language movement, the gaelicising of west Belfast, the 1991 Census, Irish in the arts, economic activity, broadcasting, prisons. Further research is needed in all these areas.

Our thanks are due to the contributors, to Colm Mac Aindreasa for knowing what buttons to push, to Séamus Ó hAnnaidh for his patience and creativity, and to Máire Bean Uí Bhruadair and Eibhlín Ní Chnáimhsí for their direct input and for keeping the show on the road when their colleagues were otherwise engaged.

Contents

Foreword	3
Living with Irish. IAN MALCOLM	7
Plus ça change: the Irish language and politics. AODÁN Mac PÓILIN	31
The very dogs in Belfast will bark in Irish The Unionist Government and the Irish language 1921-43. LIAM ANDREWS	49
Nationalists and the Irish language in Northern Ireland: Competing Perspectives. CAMILLE O'REILLY	95
Protestant learners of Irish in Northern Ireland. GORDON McCOY	131
Aspects of the Irish language movement. AODÁN Mac PÓILIN	171
Can linguistic minorities cope with a favourable majority? ANTAINE Ó DONNAILE	191
Notes on contributers	210

Living with Irish
IAN MALCOLM

Introduction

If I'd a pound (or a punt, come to that) for every time someone has said to me 'What on earth do you want to learn Irish for?' I doubt that I'd be especially wealthy. That's because people rarely ask the question of me, for the simple reason that, as an Ulster Protestant, I'm not always keen to reveal my passion for what one of our local politicians once described as 'that Leprechaun language'. In the space of two sentences, therefore, I've come to the great dilemma that faces almost every Protestant *Gaeilgeoir* in Northern Ireland: just how open can you afford to be? And that, in a nutshell, is what this essay is all about. My intention is to look at the language from a purely Protestant perspective, identifying the reasons why people like myself speak Irish, what it means to me personally and why others have a problem with it.

It's not my intention, you'll no doubt be pleased to hear, to launch into the almost traditional 'Irish is part of the Indo–European group of languages ...' style which provides such a dull introduction to so many books written on the subject. The fact that Irish is descended from the Indo–European group of languages is neither here nor there in contemporary usage. What I want to do is to celebrate the fact that we have a living, vibrant language which is more than the preserve of anthropologists and historians. Yes, the history is important – and, indeed, is something I hope to explore at a later stage in much greater detail than the confines of this essay could possibly permit – but what I'm concerned with here is this beautiful language that all of us in Northern Ireland are perfectly entitled to share, regardless of class, creed or politics. I don't particularly care what viewpoint or political soap–box you, the reader, is coming from but I hope that, at the end of this piece, you'll have a greater understanding of the language itself and why I regard it as a precious jewel in a cultural crown that can sit as easily on the head of the loyallest Loyalist as it can on that of the most ardent Republican who would claim a direct ancestral line from the Fianna. A crown it most certainly is and, the best part of all is that it fits everyone. If I can, in some small way, help persuade you, particularly if you're an Ulster Protestant, to try it out for size then I will have achieved something worthwhile.

Given that this article is primarily about myself and how I interact with the language, my political views, while irrelevant in broader terms, are inevitably of some significance and it's important right from the outset that I give at least some indication as to my allegiance. As a journalist, I feel it important that one must not identify strongly with any particular group or party. To do that, I believe, is to compromise one's integrity and professional independence. On this one occasion, and specifically for the purposes of helping to do something on behalf of the language that means so much to me, I shall put that tenet on hold. I can safely say that, no, I'm not a republican (far from it); no, I'm not a nationalist. What I am is unashamedly unionist in outlook and belief; as proud of my political tradition as I am of my linguistic heritage. With that safely out of the way (though I will return to the subject of politics and the language a little later), I now invite you to join me on a brief exploration of Irish and the Ulster Protestant. I invite you, too, to try on that crown ... you might just be surprised at how well it fits.

Why and how?

Moving right back to the beginning, why, then, did I, as an Ulster Protestant, choose to learn Irish, a language which, for many, is associated with the De Valerian dream of dancing at the crossroads, a 32–county state and direct–rule from Maynooth? Add to that the *Tiocfaidh ár lá* mantra of hard–boiled republicans who would seek to use the language as a tool for political advancement and you've got anything but a basis for mutual understanding on something that does, after all, belong to us all. As so much of our lives on this island, sadly, revolves around politics our views on other matters not connected to politics become clouded by pre-judgement and misconception. Irish has suffered in that way. To speak Irish, therefore, is perceived as being equivalent to identifying oneself as being Irish.

At the root of the widespread Protestant antipathy – and in many cases outright hostility – to the language is, I suspect, something that could be interpreted as a crisis of identity. It's not some abstract sort of 'what's it all about' kind of identity-crisis but, rather, a feeling of being caught between two distinct traditions, separated from one by the Irish Sea and from the other by a border that is both geographical and psychological. The fact that, in general, the Ulster Protestant will identify with all things British is true up to a point, but there are those parts of 'mainland' culture to which he has no claim. And, as much as I hate to denigrate anyone's culture, is it not perhaps a good thing that we can disassociate ourselves from Morris dancing, tepid beer and places with silly names like Chorlton–cum–Hardy or Ashby–de–la–Zouch.

On the other hand, I reckon we've got all the best bits – like lazy summer afternoons on the cricket field, Marks and Spencer and the right to enjoy the musical celebration of pure, unadulterated Britishness that is the Last Night of the Proms. In some ways this represents a 'pick and mix' approach to British culture but it seems logical to me to ignore those things with which I cannot identify yet at the same time embrace other aspects of the 'whole' to which I belong. To put it another way, there are many parts of Northern Ireland's own culture with which people in the south of England, for example, could not identify – like that world–renowned celebration of cholestrol which we call the Ulster fry. This 'pick and mix' approach to citizenship is not a bad thing. It makes sense and it underlines our individuality as a people. And you can see it at work on the sports field. Take rugby – come the Ireland–England match in the Five Nations championship loyal Ulster Prods will descend on Dublin, shouting their heads off for Ireland. It would be a rare Ulsterman indeed who would make the journey to Landsdowne Road to cheer on England. Using cricket as another example, the reverse is generally true and, while few Northern Ireland fans are as likely to make the pilgrimage to Lords, they'll happily support England in any test series showdown with the Aussies. This, I fancy, might have something to do with the fact that, as much as they love cricket, Ireland's team does not compete on the test stage and, therefore, loyalty is transferred to an international team that is playing for 'us'.

So what, then, is all this stuff about an identity crisis? Once you analyse just what's at issue, you can easily see that it's less of a crisis and more of an opportunity. That, then, is how I view not only Irish, but the whole question of what it means to be 'Irish'. I see it as a double opportunity to enhance my own culture through those things that appeal to me. There are many parts of 'Irish' culture that are important to me. The language and the music are, to my mind, the finest in the world. But Irish dancing? Now that's an automatic switch–off. I know every Irish dancer in the land will want to see me strung up for saying this, but I reckon your typical four–hand reel, three–legged jig or five–headed hornpipe has got about as much entertainment value as being bitten by a mosquito. In fact, the mosquito bite has probably got the edge. It might also be something to do with the fact that I am to dancing what Sadaam Hussein is to international relations. But the point is surely made: simply because I love the Irish language and its music does not mean that I must – by dint of some perceived or implied cultural obligation – embrace everything to do with that culture.

Irish sport would be another example. I'm the sort of person who will probably watch just about any sport on television –

with the possible exception of golf and the definite exception of darts – and, should a hurling or Gaelic football match happen to be on, chances are that I'll watch it. It's not that I'm particularly entranced by the sport itself. I'm not. I can watch it on TV because it's reasonable viewing but it's not something I look upon as being part of my culture. For that to happen, the Gaelic Athletic Association would have to rewrite its constitution and make football and hurling something that can bridge the two communities in Northern Ireland. I can remember many years ago, in 1977 I think, that Armagh – my home county – got through to the all–Ireland football final with Dublin. I'm certainly no expert, but I believe that was the only time Armagh ever achieved such acclaim on the 32–county stage. Even though I was still at school, I remember being amused to see 'Up the Dubs' written on a wall in a loyalist part of the town. Armagh's success in reaching the final was no source of pride to Protestants in my area and Dublin's victory in the Croke Park showdown was, if you like, the 'perfect' result. Most Protestants look upon Gaelic sports as discriminatory at best and sectarian at worst. I would find it hard to disagree.

The sports themselves probably do not go far enough back in history to take us to a point where they were something that genuinely involved everyone and every tradition on this island. The language, however, does have such a pedigree. To put it in a nutshell, I regard myself very much as being British yet at the same time I acknowledge a sense of Irishness. I'm a citizen of the United Kingdom yet the place in which I live is called Northern Ireland. To ignore this is to automatically disinherit onself from the rich veins of twin tradition that run through us all, no matter how we might view ourselves politically. Were I given the opportunity to freely state my nationality on my passport I would choose neither British nor Irish, instead settling on something that I think could sum up all aspects of my culture, my personality and my identity – Brit–Irish might be an appropriate compromise.

Before I go on to explain why I began to learn the language,

I'd first like to give some idea as to the passion and intensity of my love for Irish. When I started learning – I attended a weekly one–and–a–half–hour class for adults at Queen's University – my conversion was immediate. Straight away, I realised that Irish was not going to be a 'hobby' or something to fill out the week. It was, I knew, going to become a way of life and that is exactly what it is for me. I will admit that, yes, I am fanatical about the language. I love every idiom, every nuance, every subtlety and complexity, every grammatical construction, every word of this thing that has become such a part of me. Now I regard myself as a fairly fluent speaker and every moment of every day is spent immersed in the language. I listen to Irish language radio, I watch Irish language television, I read everything I can get my hands on in Irish and I even ring people up at all hours just to get speaking Irish to them. Even as I write this – in English, of course – my head is filled with Irish thoughts. I operate primarily in an English–speaking world but that doesn't stop me from practising my Irish at every time of the night or day. I think in Irish and I look forward to things in Irish and I reflect on the events of the day in Irish. I can do all that because Irish is a real language, a living language, a language that is changing all the time to adapt to today's world. Some people think that Irish is a mouldy old thing fossilised in time like a lump of bog oak. They believe that it can, therefore, have no space for new ideas or new technology. How wrong they are. Yes, Irish has a word for computer. Yes, Irish has a word for the Internet. And yes, Irish has a word for AIDS. If you can think of it in English, you can express it in Irish.

Irish, for me, is no idle way to while away the time. It's a way of communicating with other people both through the spoken and written word. I've been a journalist – and journalism is a profession I love – for many years but now I write in two languages instead of one. And I'm immensely proud of that fact. To be perfectly honest, I probably feel more at home writing in Irish now than I do in English and that's because I believe that, in discovering Irish, I've discovered my true self. I am one of the lucky few who has managed to lay claim to the heritage that was denied me for so many years. In terms of the language, perhaps I'm a zealot. Perhaps I'm a fanatic. But I'll tell you what, at the end of the day I'm still a Protestant and I'm still an Ulsterman.

All of which brings me back to why and how I started to learn Irish. Looking back on it now, I can see that, although I didn't realise it at the time, I was speaking Irish almost as soon as I could talk. When I learned how to say Portadown, or Ballymena, or Belfast I was speaking my first few words of Irish. I didn't realise that these placenames were simple anglicisations of the old Irish. When I was old enough to watch the Orangemen out on the Twelfth I didn't realise that the placenames on the lodge banners were as Irish as St Patrick. But I suppose I soon realised that there was more to placenames than meets the eye, for I can still recall while driving back from our annual holidays – in Donegal as it happens and, even though I didn't know it at the time, in the Gaeltacht area of Falcarragh – asking plenty of questions. I remember if, for example, we were driving through Omagh, I'd say to my dad: 'What does Omagh mean?' and then, once that question was out of the way, add in a conspiratorial whisper: 'Daddy, is this a Protestant town or a Catholic town?' With the innocence of youth, I hardly knew the difference then but sure wasn't that the sort of question that everybody in my class back at school would ask, so wasn't it only right and proper that I should do the same?

Now, leaving the religious addendum out of the way, my dad rarely let me down on the 'what does it mean?' question for he had sufficient grasp of the language to interpret placenames. Years before, he now tells me, he had learned Irish for a time. His introduction to the beauty of the language was, alas, short–lived, for when the IRA set about its border campaign he no longer felt comfortable at the classes, which were 'on the other side of the house'. That would, in fact, be a perfect illustration of how IRA violence, rather than 'uniting' anything, only serves to drive people apart. Think of it: an Ulster Protestant's attempts to learn Irish cut short by those who would lay claim to the same language.

Although my dad's grasp of the language was basic at best, I remember that he sometimes put me to bed with the words *'Oíche mhaith'* or *'Codladh sámh'*. Again, it probably didn't mean an awful lot to me at the time but looking back on it now I can see that he did more than enough to make sure that I would never be hostile to Irish. Add to that his love of Irish history and mythology – not the 1916 stuff or the 'Ireland unfree shall never be at peace' platitudes, but rather the stories of Sorley Boy Mac Donnell and the Flight of the Earls – and you can easily see why I should eventually discover the language for myself. Perhaps I'm just lucky in having a father who could bring old Erin's past to life with his storytelling skills – many were the tales he told of Doe Castle in Donegal or of Edenduffcarrick in Co Antrim – but, whatever, it showed me the door to a greater understanding of my heritage. Now, many years later, I've opened that door. And I like what I see inside.

The good, the bad, and the bigoted

Having looked at why I speak - and love - Irish, I'd like to explore the political dimension of the language in relation to Protestants in Northern Ireland. This, in effect, involves two different aspects of the whole linguistic/political issue and prompts two primary questions.

- Question one: to put it simply, what sort of a Protestant will decide to learn Irish and is there any political motivation in arriving at that decision?
- Question two: having made the decision to learn Irish, for whatever reason, what are the implications of this in purely human, purely personal terms?

Starting with the first question, the simple answer is that the reasons for learning Irish vary from person to person. If, however, we must put things into this political context – as, of course, we're very much wont to do in Northern Ireland – I would say that it's possible to identify three 'types' of Protestant who decide to learn Irish. Those falling into the first category would be people who have no hard and fast political opinions whatever. People who are, perhaps, generally disinterested in the age–old battles between unionism and nationalism or loyalism and republicanism. For them, the decision to learn Irish has nothing whatever to do with politics and the implications of learning the language are similarly divorced from the machinations of Westminster or the Dáil. Politics neither prompts their initial interest in Irish nor leads to any sort of 'discovery' that might change their views of Ireland's political geography.

This first group, I feel, might well be in the minority for, while there are many who would claim to have 'no politics', in most cases closer questioning will normally reveal some sort of political preference, no matter how gently stated that preference is. People in Northern Ireland are obsessed with trying to find out what makes the next person tick. When two strangers meet, there often appears to be an almost ritualised obligation to discover what side of the house they're from. The techniques might vary from listening carefully to how they pronounce their 'h's' and casually asking what schools they attended, to, should you find yourself in the wrong company (ie, wined–up knife–wielding thugs) 'Are you a Prod/Fenian?' In its more refined form, this time–honoured ritual takes on the elegance of a folk–dance and, who knows, might even be worthy of cross–community funding on the basis that it is an indigenous art which transcends all barriers ...

The second category would, in my mind at least, include those who, while Ulster Protestants, hold nationalist or even republican views. I know quite a few who definitely fall into this category and for them the decision to learn the language is a consciously political one. I must add, however, that most regard themselves as nationalist rather than republican. These are people who would, by choice, see themselves as Irish and feel that in learning the language they are underlining that sense of Irishness, strengthening their beliefs and making a statement about who they are. The language, for them, is part of a package that can include everything from drinking Guinness to wearing Aran sweaters at the height of summer out of a sense of national duty. They might see themselves as the inheritors of the Wolfe Tone tradition – and, in truth, there are in Northern Ireland some families who are fiercely proud of their Presbyterian ancestors' part in the 1798 rising, holding firmly to the beliefs – political and religious – of their forefathers.

The third category – and indeed the one to which I belong – includes people who have unionist beliefs of varying shades. For them, the language is a cultural inheritance that they want to reclaim, while at the same time staying totally British. This approach, as I've already said, does recognise that all of us in Ulster have access to an Irish cultural dimension that comes automatically with living on this island. But it's important to remember that it is cultural and not political. I like to think of myself as proof that one's background is no barrier whatever to learning Irish. How I vote on polling day is not relevant to the language issue; nor does the fact that I am an Irish speaker alter the way in which I cast that vote. For me, it's quite straightforward. I speak Irish because I regard it as being my language. It is by no means the intellectual property of any one section of the community. The fact that I'm not nationalist in outlook is of no consequence.

All of which brings me quite neatly to the next question: what perceptions do others have of Protestant Irish speakers? This, I expect, is one of the most important issues of all for many people who have discovered that learning Irish can have a variety of implications. It also explains why a lot of Protestants choose to remain firmly in the linguistic closet, as it were. Not terribly long ago, I was down in Dublin to meet some Irish-speaking friends, all of whom know that I value nothing more than my language. They know, too, that I hold definite unionist views and make no apologies for that. After a while, another man joined us and started chatting away, interested to learn that I was from the North. He seemed impressed with my grasp of the language and asked, quite innocently, 'I suppose you learned your Irish in the Kesh?' Linguistic stereotype number one: he clearly assumed that because I had an interest in the language I was from a republican background and had chosen to spend my time behind the wire polishing up my irregular verbs and prepositional pronouns. I'll readily admit that I have indeed 'done time for the cause'. But for me 'the cause' is the Irish language itself and 'the time' is every minute I've spent – on the outside, I hasten to add – improving my grasp of my language.

That is one illustration of how Protestant Irish speakers are perceived by others. To explore this in further depth we have to examine it from both sides. First of all, how do nationalists and republicans view the Protestant Irish speaker? Well, I reckon this varies from person to person and from place to place, but in my own experience I must say that I've never had anything but a positive response. I find that people on the nationalist and republican side are delighted to welcome the Protestant Irish speaker and again, there are several reasons for this. Very many nationalists share the belief that if a Prod is learning Irish he's already half way to being Irish in every sense of the word. It's a common mistake, but then so many – on both sides – have been conditioned to think that an interest in the language equates to an interest in nationalism. So, what happens when these people find out that I don't comply with that stereotyped view? Again, I have to say that the response has always been a positive one. The fact that I'm speaking Irish and coming from a unionist perspective appears to be something that they're very happy to accept. And I think I know why.

The reason is that people like myself show that Irish can

transcend politics, religion and belief – something that the language's mainly nationalist proponents have been trying to argue for years. Unfortunately, there's not a lot of hard proof to back up the argument but I, for one, do show that it's not entirely without justification. I've found many Falls Road Gaeilgeoirs incredibly helpful and full of encouragement, always willing to answer my never–ending questions about some grammatical point or other. Even though there's a tremendous gulf between us in political terms, when it comes to the language we are united. I always like to rationalise this one by remembering that it's just as easy to say 'to Hell with the Pope' in Irish as it is to say 'F**k the Queen' in English. The language is there to be used by all and, should people want to use it for futile, petty sloganising they have that choice – it's not the fault of the language. It is worth saying however, that I have a lot of contact with Irish speakers of every persuasion in my capacity as a journalist so I'm not, I suppose, meeting other Gaeilgeoirs 'cold'. In conclusion, though, I can say that the majority of Gaeilgeoirs I've met 'on the other side' are genuinely pleased to see someone who's both Protestant and unionist taking an interest in the language.

It's not, alas, quite so cut and dried when we examine how other Protestants view that minority of their co–religionists who have decided to learn Irish. As I've already indicated, many Protestants who speak the language tend to keep their interest under wraps, not because it's something they're ashamed of but because they know that it can have consequences over which they have no control. If for example, you live in a strongly loyalist area it's highly unlikely that you're going to openly declare undying love for the Irish language or set up classes in the community centre. Nor are you likely to put the little 'I love Gaeilge' sticker on the windscreen of your car when the daily jaunt down to the shops takes you past the local Orange hall. It's very important that we don't get into vague generalisations which give the impression that the majority of Protestants are hostile to the idea of someone they know learning Irish. That's not true at all, but it must be said that an intolerant minority do have very definite views ... and being nice to Irish–speakers is not one of them. Being a journalist means that I can probably be more open than most about my interest in the language from a professional viewpoint. On a personal level, though, it's a different ball game and caution has to be the watchword, although the usual responses are harmless enough, such as: 'What do you want to learn THAT for?'; 'You must be really clever.'; 'You'll be entering the priesthood next, eh?'; 'I'd like to learn it myself but it looks really hard.'; 'The only Irish I know is Bórd na Móna peat briquettes.' All fairly typical of the more positive responses the Protestant Irish speaker is likely to enounter. Hardly the stuff of nightmares and cold sweats. Indeed, I quite enjoy the banter of people asking me to translate The Sash into Irish.

Unfortunately though, there is a darker side, as this grim little selection shows: 'You want to watch yourself'; 'If you like Irish so much why don't you go and live in Dublin'; 'Turncoat/Lundy/Traitor'; 'I've no time for that oul foreign language'; 'I know where you live' (always muttered in a darkly threatening manner) and as much as I'm revolted by these remarks I can to an extent understand why some feel threatened by the language. To them, it is inextricably intertwined with nationalism and republicanism; years of conditioning have led them to believe that Irish is a cultural weapon brandished by those who would seek to drive honest Ulstermen into a land of Popery and subjugation. A lot of people on both sides share the blame for this and it is an issue too complex to explore right now but one which I hope to cover in detail at a later stage. Suffice to say, though, that a lot of people who despise the language are descended from Irish or *Gàidhlig* (Scots–Gaelic) speakers – and you don't always have to go back to Plantation times to find this out. One person I know, for example, harangued me for daring to speak 'that foreign tongue' within his earshot but, in more conciliatory mood several days later, admitted that his own grandfather was an Irish speaker. It was a reluctant acceptance that Irish had played some part in his family history. Whether he liked it or not, he was at least prepared to admit to it. Proof, in my view, that, with a lot of hard work, Irish can be freed from the shackles of perception and given back to those to whom it belongs. Everyone.

I think it's worth making brief reference to another set of responses, this time from people (obviously Catholics) who studied Irish at school but found it not to their taste. Many of them are as hostile to the language as the bitterest loyalist, albeit for entirely different reasons. They're astounded that anyone – particularly a Protestant – should be remotely interested in something they detest. 'I hated Irish' is a refrain that I hear time and time again from people who, to my mind, had an opportunity that was never given to me. I wish that I'd had the chance to learn Irish when I was at school. But then again I'm looking at the language with total passion and I have to realise that it would be unreasonable for me to expect everyone to share that passion. Just because someone is a Catholic or indeed a nationalist doesn't mean that they're automatically going to love Irish. It's all a matter of individual freedom and everyone has the right to choose.

Looking to the future

Inevitably, an essay of this kind is going to come back to one basic question: what next for the Irish language?

Given the phenomenal growth of interest in Irish in recent years - and Belfast has played no insignificant part in that new revival – I think we can say that the future of the language is indeed secure. Despite the fact that the 'true Gaeltacht' areas are under pressure from a variety of sources (a Gaeltacht is an area in which Irish is spoken as the first language; a Galltacht is an area in which English is spoken as the first language) more people are speaking the language now than for a very long time which prompts me to ask two more questions. Is this 'Galltacht' Irish inferior to that spoken in Gaoth Dobhair or Oileán

Chléire? And just where do Ulster Protestants fit into this picture of a language apparently in the full bloom of revival?

Dealing with the first question – the validity of non-Gaeltacht Gaelic – I have to say that there is probably a minority which does indeed view, say, Belfast Irish as some unpure creature skulking along the margins of the 'real language'. These are the linguistic purists who, you'll often discover, believe that the only 'true Irish' comes not even from a single Gaeltacht but a tiny area within that. You know, 'the third house by the fourth bend in the wee river of the big glen is where you'll find the best Irish in Ireland'. I think it means that they are missing out on the broader picture and losing touch with the Irish language as it is spoken today, but I have to admire their dedication. Grammatically and aesthetically, 'Belfast Irish' might be vile when compared with the old Irish of the Blue Stack Mountains or the richness of Ros Goill but it works. And if people are speaking Irish as an everyday language, it's clear that they're going to adapt it to their own needs.

There are people in Belfast who frown when I greet them with *'Cén chaoi a bhfuil tú?'*, a different form of 'How are you?', when they've been conditioned to expect the Ulster *'Cad é mar atá tú?'* Why? What difference does it make? We're all speaking the same language and those who restrict themselves to one dialect on some obscure point of principle are indeed not seeing the full picture. It's learning and speaking the language that's important at the end of the day, not what version one chooses to speak and indeed, this brings me to another point altogether – each Gaeltacht has its own *cora cainte*, expressions, sayings and idioms peculiar to a particular area that have been built up over hundreds of years. Gaeltacht 'outsiders' might not have this linguistic armoury at their disposal but I suspect that, as the Northern Ireland – and I use the term Northern Ireland deliberately – revival develops, this 'new' Irish will become equally enriched, albeit in a totally 'Ulster' way. The language is changing all the time and to survive in a world dominated by what I call the 'Coca Cola culture' – that global takeover by the marketing superpowers whose products and ideas have become almost a language in their own right – it has to.

Some 40 or 50 years ago the language underwent a complete 'make–over' (for want of a more descriptive term), with significant changes, particularly in regard to the spelling of words, that immediately made it more approachable. There were, I'm sure, those who were appalled at such tinkering but nowadays we have a language that is a lot less daunting for the learner. The 'universality' of the *Caighdeán Oifigiúil*, as it's known, has done much to promote understanding of Irish and it has cut down a lot of the barriers between dialects. The critics would claim that it has funnelled Irish into a narrow channel where much of the language's breadth has been lost but I would have to disagree. If by losing a little of that 'breadth' the language has suffered, by the same token it has been given new breadth in that it's so much more amenable and while the *Caighdeán* indeed standardised spelling it didn't, as some claim, butcher the language. There are throughout Irish many idioms and constructions that, while outside the patronage of the *Caighdeán,* remain in everyday use. In other words, what happened was that while the *Caighdeán* did everyone a favour in ironing out some of the complexities of the language it could not steamroller those things that have genuine value. All of which, to my mind, leaves us with a leaner, fitter language geared towards a new millennium.This is where the comparison between Irish and Scots Gaelic comes in. The two languages are fundamentally the same. For example: In Ulster Irish I say *'Cad é mar atá tú?'* (How are you?). In *Gàidhlig* (Scots Gaelic) I say *'Ciamar a thà thù?'*. You can see how close the two 'languages' are ... indeed, it's more a question of dialect.

Scots Gaelic, however, has not undergone the reformation that its Irish counterpart enjoyed and consequently, in my view, is much more difficult to learn. While the constructions are in many ways similar, the spellings are archaic and if I was a *Gàidhlig*–speaking Scot with an interest in promoting my language, I'd be crying out for changes. Roman type won the day over the old Irish script as well and that's another thing that has been a move for the better because everyone understands it from the day they're first able to read. Even so, old Irish – in both form and type – still has its place and, while my Irish is modern in every form, I love to read books written in the old script. The text is an art in itself. And while there have been many changes to the language in the past 50 years and it's just as likely that the next 50 will see many more it is not something to be worried about – it's simply a natural, and essential, development. To put it another way: in order to keep something of greater value, it is sometimes necessary to lose other things of lesser worth, sad though we might be to see them go.

I have digressed a fair bit so I will return to the central issue of this essay: what about the Ulster Protestant in relation to the Irish language? How can more Protestants be encouraged to take up an interest in Irish? Where can they learn? Is there anything to give us hope that more Protestants even want to learn the language? And while I'm not sure that I even have answers to these questions I do believe that there are many people out there who would take an active interest in their language with a minimum of encouragement. I've spoken to many who tell me they'd like to learn. And I've spoken to a few who've even made a tentative attempt to do so.

Some time ago, when the BBC broadcast 'Now You're Talking', an Irish language series for learners many Protestants got their first real taste of the language because here was an entertaining, well–produced programme that educated and informed. I had only started learning a few months before at that time and, as you can guess, it was immediately essential viewing in my house. As I've said, it was entertaining, it was modern, it was everything a language programme should be. But it was more than that. In 'Now You're Talking' I believe we have something that genuinely crossed the divide because it didn't put the language into an 'Irish' context.

Watching the series (and I only missed two episodes), I saw

nothing that could have given offence to anyone in terms of religion or politics and, believe me, I watched very carefully. In every episode I couldn't help but keep a wary eye out for sacred pictures: I saw none. I examined the characters to see if they were wearing crucifixes: I saw none. I scanned the walls for 'Up the IRA' graffiti: I saw none. So, unless there were priests, nuns and Provos swigging holy water like there was no tomorrow in the two programmes that I didn't see, I think I can say that 'Now You're Talking' marked a major step forward in at least introducing Protestants to the language. There was nothing to give the programme any particular flavour other than that of a well–conceived and well–executed effort to teach the language in a simple, direct manner. The beauty of 'Now You're Talking' is that, being a TV programme, you could watch it from the comfort of your own sofa, taking your first steps in Irish without having to go out through your front door. From a Protestant perspective, it was ideal ... you could learn Irish and no–one would ever know. I've absolutely no idea how many Protestants were regular 'Now You're Talking' viewers, but I'll wager it was more than a few.

Assuming, however, that as a Protestant who watched 'Now You're Talking' and got some sort of grounding in the language, just where would you go from there. For some, a cassette–based 'listening' course might have been the next step. Again, these enable the learner to study the language at home, in a safe, relaxed environment. Great though this is – and I don't care how people begin to learn the language, just so long as they do – the great challenge now for those actively involved in promoting the Irish language is to recreate that safe, relaxed environment outside the home. This, I believe, really is the key to making Irish more appealing to Protestants in general. But how do you achieve this?

If you're a Catholic you're going to have no problem in finding suitable classes in your own area where you'll feel very much at home, learning alongside people you know. Can you do that as a Protestant? The answer, plainly, has to be no, on the basis that very few classes are run in Protestant areas. Some Protestants do go across the divide to learn the language but this would be a tiny minority. While there's a world of classes on offer to everyone in west Belfast, not many Protestants are going to feel totally at ease there. Conversely, most teachers of Irish would be Catholics and they're going to feel equally uncomfortable going into, say, east Belfast, to hold classes.

Others have already identified the problem as being a lack of 'neutral venues' where everyone, Protestant and Catholic, can feel at home. Let's not worry too much about setting up classes in Protestant areas for that's not going to happen in any significant way quite yet. The 'neutral venue' is the key, a place where people aren't worried about who they're sitting next to or what foot the person at the front of the class kicks with. Somewhere like central Belfast is ideal and several highly successful classes do take place in the city, giving Protestants an equal opportunity to learn their language. In Ulster's towns, however, it might not be quite so easy as people do not have the anonymity of the city but, assuming that a suitably neutral venue can be identified, the possibilities are there. Encouraging Protestants to go to Irish classes is the first step but it must be stated categorically that this is something which cannot be forced or imposed. The will to learn the language must be there at the outset. We have already outlined the many reasons why Protestants might feel inclined to learn Irish in the first place. If they have that will, if they've made that decision, then, provided that they're not having to take any perceived risks, they'll be happy to go along to classes. It's up to those of us who already speak Irish and want to encourage others to do the same to make it easy for those Protestants with an interest in the language to do so at their own pace and, most importantly, on their own terms, whatever those terms might be.

'Now You're Talking' is one specific example of a particular concept that has opened new doors on our language to people of every persuasion. Another example would be *Oideas Gael* in Glencolumkille, one of the loveliest, yet most isolated, parts of

Donegal. It has deservedly won international acclaim for its efforts in promoting the Irish language. Religion and politics do not come into the equation and that, I think, is part of the reason why it attracts many Ulster Protestants every summer. Indeed, the whole idea was conceived by a Co Donegal Catholic, Liam Ó Cuinneagáin, and a Belfast man of Presbyterian stock, Dr Seosamh Watson. From humble beginnings, the college – strictly for adults and catering for everyone from complete beginner to those fine-tuning their language skills – has grown into something that is at the leading edge of Irish language development.

Using the most up-to-date teaching methods (you can forget learning by rote or compulsory verb tables) *Oideas Gael* works well at every level, not only in the classroom but by adding a social element to study. And this social element is hugely important from a Protestant perspective. Many of them will have been learning the language in isolation, not having had the chance to put what they know into practice. At *Oideas Gael*, however, they meet people from all over the world in what has been rightly described as a 'global village'. All of a sudden, they're able to use Irish as a 'real' language, doing the simple things – like ordering a cup of coffee or commenting on the weather. They've effectively made the move from textbook theory to the real world. Very often, *Oideas Gael* has another surprise in store: many 'first-timers' go along thinking they're the only Protestant in Ulster with an interest in Irish ... until they discover the person sitting next to them in the class is a loyal Prod from Portadown, Ballymena or wherever. *Oideas Gael* has succeeded in creating its own neutral environment, where religion and politics are not matters for discussion.

If 'Now You're Talking' and *Oideas Gael* are positive developments, there, are unfortunately, still many negative influences around that do little to encourage the Protestant learner. In terms of learning material, for example, a lot of the standard textbooks come from the days when teachers and scholars looked upon Irish as a Catholic language for a Catholic people. Many of the older grammar books were written by priests and, as someone who has read quite a few by dint of my fascination with grammar, I can only conclude that they were never intended for Protestant eyes. In some, spiritual direction seems to take precedence over the language itself. Even more recent texts, alas, are not free from Catholic overtones, with frequent references to Mass, priests and the Church.

Such books are set in a world where every little boy (Seán, naturally) plays hurling, every little girl (Máire, of course) plays camogie and every big brother (Séamus, who else?) is a priest working in the overseas missions. Dad, meanwhile, is looking forward to the all–Ireland final and mum is getting ready for the parish bingo. I suppose this approach could be given a Prod–friendly revamp in which the little boy (wee Sam) is a brilliant cricketer, the little girl (Sharon) is very good at hockey and big brother (Billy) is on coastal duty in Bahrain with the Royal Navy. Dad, meanwhile, is watching the big Rangers game on telly and mum's making sandwiches for the church fête. The real way forward, of course, is to dispense with stereotypes altogether and it's encouraging to see that the most recent textbooks are more universally acceptable. Things are changing at last and teaching methods, too, are changing, with the communicative approach taking precedence over old–style 'bang it into their thick skulls at any price' approach which put many pupils off Irish for life in years gone by.

For the moment, though, this may be a purely academic matter from the Protestant perspective when Irish is not a subject in state schools. It effectively brings me to one final question: will Protestants ever get the chance to learn Irish at school in Northern Ireland? First of all, imagine what would happen if Irish lessons were made compulsory in state schools. There would, to put it mildly, be uproar. Until such times as Protestants in general become aware of their own ties – historic and contemporary – with the language, Irish can not play a formal part in the state school curriculum. Indeed, I firmly believe that Irish must never be forced on anyone, regardless of religion. As I've already said, just because I love the language does not mean everyone else is going to share my passion. I accept that. But at the same time I see ways in which young people could be given an introduction to the language – if they wish. Others have suggested that Irish could be a curriculum option at Upper Sixth level, in the same way that subjects like Japanese already are in some schools. No-one would be forced to learn Irish, but the choice would be there.

Integrated schools do come into the equation too, and here there is likely to be less parental resistance to the idea of Protestant children at least getting an introduction to the language. The education system might have a great role to play in the future but for now I think those of us with an interest in the language should be more concerned with small steps than giant leaps. It's by encouraging those who are now taking their first steps in Irish that real progress will come ... and everyone who has the language's best interests at heart will be ready to meet that challenge.

Conclusion

I hope I've demonstrated beyond all doubt that there's no reason whatever why a Protestant (unionist, loyalist or whatever) should not regard the Irish language as his or her own. Irish is my language. It's a language that I feel both proud and privileged to speak. Irish has, I suppose, changed many things in my life – for the better – but it has not altered my 'core values' in any way and why should it? It could be like that for everyone. Just because you can say *'Go raibh maith agat'* doesn't mean you forget the words of 'God Save The Queen'. Just because you can say *'Cad é mar atá tú'* doesn't mean you have to join in every time you hear a song that mentions 'green, white and gold'. A point of information for those who don't know the difference: the colours of the flag are not green, white and gold, but green, white and orange. That's how it's always been. The 'gold' only came into the picture because republican-minded songwriters couldn't find anything to rhyme with orange and they discovered that their ditties weren't scanning too well. But with gold you can make just about anything rhyme ... heroes bold, Fenian men of old, their stories they are told etc. (Try it with orange, by the way, and I guarantee you'll be climbing the walls – or flagpole). So bear in mind that every time you hear a song which mentions 'green, white and gold' you are, in fact, being sold a musical lie. Puts a slightly different perspective on 'The Dying Rebel' don't you think?

I don't know if the arguments that I've put forward in this essay will convince you to take that first step on the road to becoming an Irish speaker. That's your choice, not mine. Irish is an entity in its own right. It doesn't come as part of a 'boxed set', with free rosary beads, tricolour bedspread and the option on a half–price annual subscription to *An Phoblacht*. True, for some, Irish is part of a political package deal but it doesn't have to be that way and even if I haven't persuaded you to rush out and seize the opportunity to reclaim something that belongs to us all, I hope that you might at least look differently upon the language. Even if you prefer not to acknowledge it as a part of your own history and heritage perhaps you can now understand that it's not something to be frightened of or hostile towards.

Irish is all around us, even in the way we use English. 'Smashing' is a word derived from the Gaelic expression *Is maith sin*. Even though you might not realise it, you're speaking Irish already. Irish is our language, 'our' meaning Protestant, Catholic and Dissenter. Let's all enjoy it.

Is í ár dteanga í. Tá sé in am dúinn go léir sult a bhaint as an rud álainn seo atá againn go léir. Téigh amach agus déan é. An Ghaeilge go deo.

Plus ça change: the Irish language and politics
AODÁN MAC PÓILIN

'*We are Ulster-Scots descended from a proud and fiercely independent people with a longer tradition than that promoted by nationalists. Their language is a dead language for a dead people*'. (Jim Shannon, Democratic Unionist Party Councillor, *Irish News*, 25 - 9 - 1996)

'*We have a language worthy of value in its own right. ... We are Ulster-Scots, descended from a fiercely independent ancestry - from Scots Presbyterianism*'. (Jim Shannon, *Northern Ireland Forum: Record of Debate*, 10 - 1 - 1997, 41)

'*Is í an Ghaeilge teanga náisiúnta, dhúchasach an phobail náisiúnaigh sna Sé Chontae*'. [*Irish is the national, native language of the nationalist community in the Six Counties*].' (Máirtín Ó Muilleoir, former Sinn Féin Councillor, letter to Tony Worthington, Minister of State for Education, 1 - 9 - 1997)

In Northern Ireland, identities tend to come in packages. There is sufficient correspondence between political and religious affiliations to allow generalisations such as 'Catholic/ nationalist' and 'Protestant/unionist' to be useful, and sometimes meaningful simplifications. Political scientists squabble profitably among themselves about whether our current troubles are best defined as a religious conflict expressed in political terms or a political conflict with a powerful religious dimension.

Although cultural identity tends to be more porous, there are those who instinctively define the Irish language in terms of the polarities of the political debate. In the above quotations Mr Ó Muilleoir, a nationalist, Catholic, Irish language enthusiast with an English surname (Miller), appears to agree with Mr Shannon, a unionist, Protestant, enthusiastic speaker of Ulster Scots with an Irish Gaelic surname (Ó Seanáin), that linguistic and political (and in Mr Shannon's case, religious) allegiance are inseparable.

It is this perceived link between politics and linguistic loyalty that I wish to examine here. The perception is not entirely without foundation: Irish-speakers in Northern Ireland tend to belong overwhelmingly to the Catholic, and probably nationalist, end of the spectrum. Fewer than one in twenty of those knowing Irish and identifying their religion in the 1991 Census were Protestant (Census 1992, 159). At the same time, many of that minority of Catholic nationalists who are interested in Irish dispute the automatic association of the language with a political position. In their rhetoric, at least, they claim to believe that the language is a cultural resource which belongs equally to everyone living on the island of Ireland, nationalist and unionist, Catholic and Protestant. This perspective is shared by a small number of Protestant nationalists and an equally small number of Protestant unionists who have developed an approach to the language issue in which support for Irish co-exists with support for the political link with Britain.

On the other hand, most unionists in Northern Ireland see the Irish language movement as being inseparable from Irish nationalism.

What I have set out to do here is to try to identify what gave rise to such a fundamental divergence of perceptions in our own time. It should be noted at this point that the present unionist discomfort with and resistance to the Irish language is of recent date. When Queen Victoria came to Belfast in 1849, she noted in her diary:

> I have all along forgotten to say that the favourite motto written up on most of the arches, etc., and in every place was *'Céad Míle Fáilte'* which means 'a hundred thousand welcomes' in Irish. ... They often called out *'Céad Míle Fáilte'* and it appears in every sort of shape (Blaney 1991, 38).

In a way, we should not be surprised at the burgers of Belfast using Irish to express their loyalty to the Crown. Nineteenth century Ireland saw no necessary conflict between a cultural identity which was Irish and a political identity which was British. In fact, Irish was fashionable in Belfast in the 19th century. The inscription on the Belfast Lord Mayor's chain is in Irish - *Erin go bragh* (Ireland for ever). The foundation stone of what became the Royal Victoria Hospital was bilingual - Latin and Irish. The first society ever to have as its aim the preservation of Irish as a living language was founded in Belfast in 1830, more than sixty years before the founding of the Gaelic League. All the leaders of the language movement in Belfast, James McDonnell, Samuel Bryson, William Neilson, Robert McAdam, were Protestants, and, as far as I can make out, none of them appear to have been political nationalists. The youngest of these, McAdam, did not die until 1895, the year the first branch of the Gaelic League was founded in Belfast.

But if we examine the period between, say, 1885 and 1915, we will see the development of a significant change in perception. The language movement at the beginning of this period involved people of every political persuasion. It was also weak and ineffectual. By the end of the period, we can see a powerful and influential mass movement which was effectively controlled by the most radical wing of the nationalist movement, and in which unionist involvement was almost invisible.

At this point, I would like to dig a bit deeper into the multiple meanings of that slithery term 'political'. Politics, in spite of the best efforts of its practitioners, still means more than gaining and exercising power, and continues to carry nuances of citizenship which are rooted in concepts of civic and communal responsibility. Any group which organises itself to influence and change society is engaged in activity which is essentially political. The feminist movement speaks, accurately, of 'gender politics'. In that sense, a movement to maintain and revive a language is political.

However, in Northern Ireland today, and throughout the island during the period under discussion, the term also refers to the issue of the constitutional relationship between Great

Britain and Ireland: unionists favouring the maintenance of the political link with Britain, nationalists favouring independence from Britain. In the tiny space remaining, 'politics' can mean what it means in much of the rest of the world, party political head-butting over who should serve society, control society, or benefit from the spoils of power. Conventional party politics can be complicated by two kinds of disciplined organisations, those which attempt to influence party politics by infiltration, and those who bypass political structures through revolution. In Ireland at the turn of the century, the Irish Republican Brotherhood, commonly referred to as the Fenians, was both a revolutionary organisation and one which operated by infiltrating other organisations.

The Gaelic League was founded in 1893 to promote the Irish language in Ireland, and has always claimed to be non-political. This claim has often depended on selective use of the various overlapping senses of 'political' outlined above. It was, inevitably, political in the sense of being a single-issue pressure-group, but its claim to be non-political can be justified in the sense that the organisation avoided, for a long time, becoming embroiled in party politics. Its relationship with the ideology of Irish nationalism, however, is more complex, and is worth examining in detail.

The League was formed in response to Douglas Hyde's famous 1892 lecture, 'The Necessity for De-Anglicising Ireland'. Hyde was the son of a Church of Ireland rector from Roscommon, and was President of the League from 1893 to 1915. He had, and still has, the reputation of being a non-political figure, partly because of his stand in the Gaelic League crisis of 1915, which will be discussed later, and partly because of his recurrent claims that the League was non-political. In that context, what he had to say in 1892 is worth examining.

Hyde's arguments can be broadly divided into two main themes. One of these argues for the value of Irish in terms of cultural continuity. In 1901 he summarised that strand of his argument neatly: 'The Gaelic League is the only body in Ireland which realised that Ireland had a past, had a history, had a literature, and the only body in Ireland which sought to render the present a rational continuation of the past' (Hyde 1901, dedication). His formulation in the 1892 lecture unfortunately uses the word 'race', but it is clear that Hyde, the descendant of a Cromwellian settler, is talking about culture rather than blood: 'I believe that it is our Gaelic past which, though the Irish race does not recognise it just at present, is really at the bottom of the Irish heart.' (Hyde 1894, 121) '... do what it may, the race of today cannot wholly divest itself from the mantle of its own past' (*ibid.*, 124).

If we examine these statements in the context of their intellectual and ideological environment, we can see a close connection with a tradition rooted in the ideas of the 18th century German historian Herder, widely recognised as the father of cultural nationalism. (The symbiotic relationship between cultural and political nationalism is too big a question to begin to discuss here). We can also see in these quotations an element of essentialism, the belief that the essence, or soul, of Irishness is to be found in the Irish language. In his summary of the speech in his autobiography, written in Irish, Hyde made this explicit: 'The soul of Ireland, I said, was in that great mass of people ... who were the Irish nation ... who had Irish as their language ...' (Hyde 1931, 33).

The second thread of Hyde's argument concentrates entirely on political nationalism. He argued that Irish nationalists, as nationalists, should support the language because the preservation of Irish was the most effective defense of her cultural distinctiveness, and therefore of her nationality:

> I wish to show you that in Anglicising ourselves wholesale we have thrown away with a light heart the best claim we have upon the world's recognition of us as a separate nationality. What did Mazzini say? What is Goldwin Smith never tired of declaiming? What do the Spectator and Saturday Review harp on? That we ought to be content as an integral part of

the United Kingdom because we have lost the robes of nationality, our language and customs.

It has always been very curious to me how Irish sentiment sticks in this half-way house - how it continues to apparently hate the English, and the same time continues to imitate them; how it continues to clamour for recognition as a distinct nationality, and at the same time throws away with both hands what would make it so. If Irishmen only went a little further they would become good Englishmen in sentiment also. ... It is a fact, and we must face it as a fact, that although they adopt English habits and copy England in every way, the great bulk of Irishmen and Irishwomen over the whole world are known to be filled with a dull, ever-abiding animosity against her, and right or wrong, to grieve when she prospers, and joy when she is hurt. ... It is just because there appears no earthly chance of their becoming good members of the Empire that I urge that they should not remain in the anomalous position they are in, but since they absolutely refuse to become one thing, that they become the other: cultivate what they have rejected, and build up an Irish nation on Irish lines (Hyde 1894, 119-20).

If Hyde was, as is sometimes claimed, an apolitical figure, or even a cultural, rather than a political nationalist, why, then, does this lecture reflect political nationalism so strongly. I think that there may be two explanations. In the first place, Hyde himself was a nationalist, who had secretly supported the Fenians in his youth. In his memoirs he refers to his unsuccessful attempts to convert James Goodman, Professor of Irish in Trinity College Dublin, to nationalism (Hyde 1931, 60). But there is another explanation. The Gaelic League was partially modeled on the Gaelic Athletic Association, which had been founded shortly before, in 1884. Hyde recognised that the strength of the GAA was to have harnessed nationalist energy to the promotion of Gaelic sports, and it is likely that he saw the nationalist impulse as the most effective way for the Irish language revival to become a mass movement.

However, as well as harnessing the energies of both political and cultural nationalism, Hyde also claimed that 'this is no political matter', and attempted to appeal to unionists: 'This [the revival of Irish] is a question which most Irishmen will naturally look at from a National point of view, but it is one which ought also to claim the sympathies of every intelligent Unionist, and which, as I know, does claim the sympathy of many' (Hyde 1894, 117-8). This perspective is undermined by his west of Ireland contempt for Ulster unionists: 'In two points only was the continuity of Irishism in Ireland damaged. First in the north-east of Ulster, where the Gaelic race was expelled and the land planted with aliens, whom our dear mother Erin, assimilative as she is, has hitherto found it difficult to absorb ...' (*ibid.*, 127), followed by: 'In spite of the little admixture of Saxon blood in the north-east corner, this island *is* and will *ever* remain Celtic at the core ...' (*ibid.*, 159).

Within the ideology of the League there was, from the beginning, an unresolved conflict between non-political rhetoric and the nationalist subtext which underpinned both Hyde's own ideology and that of many of his followers. By sheer force of repetition, supplemented by the magic of his attractive personality, and an extraordinary ability to fudge contentious issues, Hyde managed for a considerable time to disguise some of the political implications of the language movement. Up to a point, he was successful. A number of prominent unionists, including a sprinkling of liberal aristocrats and clergy, became involved in the language movement in its early years. The League also attracted figures such as the Reverend Richard Kane, Grand Master of the Belfast Orange Lodge and organiser of the Anti-Home Rule Convention of 1892 who was a patron of the Belfast Branch of the League, and Lindsay Crawford, Grand Master of the Independent Orange Order, who actually stood for election to the executive committee of the League. In 1898, the League took its non-political principle so seriously that it did not participate in the unveiling in Dublin of a monument to Wolf Tone (Ó Huallacháin 1994, 57). The following statement was written in 1906 by one member of the executive committee of the League, the Reverend J Hannay, a Church of Ireland clergyman and popular novelist who wrote under the pen name of George A Birmingham:

> I myself claim to be a Loyalist, that is to say I believe King Edward to be by right and in fact Sovereign of this Kingdom of Ireland ... Quite possibly, though I do not know this, I am one of a minority in the League. But ... my principles and my opinions have made no difference whatever to my position in the League ... and I can safely assert that a similar welcome awaits anyone who, holding opinions like mine, is yet anxious for the preservation of the Irish language, and is willing to work for it, leaving aside all political questions (Ó Huallacháin 1991, 109).

The monument to Tone was actually organised by a body which acted as a front for the militantly republican IRB, and it is claimed that the 1798 celebrations were critical to the revival of that organisation. The IRB had already attempted to take over the GAA and was soon to infiltrate Sinn Féin, which in its early stages was neither republican nor militaristic. The subliminal nationalism of the Gaelic League made it an organisation which could provide perfect cover for IRB activities, as is clear from Seán T Ó Ceallaigh's description of how he used his position as business manager of the League's paper *An Claidheamh Soluis* to promote the IRB as early as 1903:

> When working for *An Claidheamh Soluis* in the early years I had an opportunity to do a lot for the IRB. ... I used to go around the country to *feiseanna* trying to increase sales of the paper, and, of course I met many young people of my own age in the different towns ... and I recruited young men for the IRB in every one of them (Ó Huallacháin 1994, 62).

There was already an instinctive resistance to the League from some unionists who were themselves enthusiastic supporters of the language. W B Yeats records that the Gaelic scholar Standish Hayes O'Grady refused to have anything to do with the League on the grounds that it was a 'Fenian organisation' (Breathnach, Ní Mhurchú 1990, 110). As the nationalist impulse behind the

League became more obvious in the early years of this century, and in particular when the League began to work closely with the Catholic Church, partly to gain its support for the teaching of Irish in schools, unionists began to find themselves more and more isolated within the language movement. Hannay soon recognised what was going on, and resigned from the League in 1907, writing a private letter to Hyde to explain his reasons:

> I take the Sinn Féin position to be the natural and inevitable development of the League principles. ... I do not myself believe that you will be able to stride the fence much longer. ... I think the movement you started will go on, whether you lead it or take the part of poor Frankenstein who created a monster he could not control (Ó Huallacháin 1991, 110).

In the event, Hyde lasted another eight years. During that period the relationship between the League and the nationalist movement became ever more clear, and ever less ambiguous. It was, for example in the League's paper *An Claidheamh Soluis* that Eoin Mac Néill, co-founder with Hyde of the Gaelic League, published his article, 'The North Began'. This article led to the founding of the Irish Volunteers, an armed organisation formed as a nationalist counterweight to the Ulster Volunteer Force. In other words, whatever success Hyde and his followers within the League had of attracting unionists to the language movement in the early years, fewer and fewer unionists could now find any space within the movement. As a further complication, unionism was itself undergoing a process of redefinition, and was beginning, partly in reaction to nationalist ideology, to move away from an Irish unionism towards a unionism which rejected any form of Irish cultural identity.

At this stage, another conflict began within the League. The radical nationalists - Sinn Féin, now moving towards a more militant stance, and the IRB - began to assert themselves within the organisation in reaction to the home rule crisis. Hyde himself was accused variously of supporting John Redmond's constitutional nationalist Irish Parliamentary Party, and of being a unionist. It is difficult to know which of these accusations represented the greatest insult. In an article in *An Claidheamh Soluis* in July 1913, Hyde attempted to explain his position:

> ... making friends all round, and getting the whole country, priests and people, Parliamentarians, Sinn Féiners, O'Brienites and Unionists, to bring pressure to bear upon big and vital issues, specially upon our education boards, so as to accomplish Irish-Ireland changes according as we are ripe for them ... (Ó Huallacháin 1991, 65).

The most comprehensive response to this perspective came in an article in the republican paper *Irish Freedom* in September:

> The work of the Gaelic League is to prevent the assimilation of the Irish nation by the English nation ... That work is as essentially anti-English as the work attempted by Fenianism or the Society of United Irishmen.

The article continues:

> The Gaelic League does not stand to take sides in the political differences that separate [nationalist] Irishmen into different parties, and therefore it is claimed to be non-political. This claim can only be upheld by twisting the plain meaning of the words. The claim ... may have misled a few unionists into the Gaelic League and to that extent may appear to be useful, but in practice it is only misleading... It has undoubtedly led some unthinking Nationalists into great confusion. It has confused the one straight issue for them, and that straight issue is whether the Irish nation or the English nation is to predominate in Ireland. ... The Irish language is a political weapon of the first importance against English encroachment (Ó Huallacháin 1994, 66/7).

I know of no better definition than this of the radical nationalist perspective on the language. The implication of defining Irish as an 'anti-English' 'political weapon of the first importance' appears to be that the function of the language movement was to assist the political movement.

By this point, Hyde's fight to leave a space for unionists within the language movement was as good as lost. The main area of struggle was now between those who were trying to keep the League open to all nationalists, and those who were attempting to use it for one section of nationalists. This is the third kind of political activity I was referring to earlier, the politics of a party or of a sub-party.

The issue was decided at the Annual General Meeting of the League held in Dundalk in 1915. Rumours were circulated that John Redmond's nationalist party intended to take the League over in the same way it had earlier attempted to take over the Irish Volunteers. Diarmuid Lynch of the IRB organised a coup. This is how he describes it in his memoirs:

> ... I communicated with prominent Gaelic Leaguers throughout the country - who were also IRB men - urging that delegates favourable to our political views should without fail be selected to attend at Dundalk ... Nominations were made accordingly ... the new Coiste [executive committee] was safe from the IRB viewpoint (Ó Huallacháin 1994, 68/9).

It is said that Hyde resigned as President of the League when its Constitution was amended to include a 'Free, Gaelic Ireland' among its objectives. Colmán Ó Huallacháin disputes this, and it may be worth our while to examine closely what happened on that historic occasion. Seán T Ó Ceallaigh records in his memoirs that he was approached by Thomas Clarke and Seán Mac Diarmada to persuade the McHale Branch of the League to propose a motion that the League should support political freedom for Ireland. The following is the text of the McHale motion:

> that the Gaelic League shall be strictly non-political and non-sectarian, and shall devote itself to realising the ideal of a Gaelic-speaking and independent Irish nation, free from all subjection to foreign influences (*ibid*, 68/9).

When a number of delegates objected to this motion on the

grounds that the second part of the proposal was as political as the first part was not, Colonel Moore proposed the following amendment:

> that the Gaelic League shall be strictly non-political and non-sectarian, and shall devote itself solely to realising the dawn of a free Gaelic-speaking Ireland *(ibid)*.

Hyde expressed his unease with the use of the word 'free', saying: 'I would consider that a political resolution, if it means that Ireland should be free from British rule'. He did, however, accept Moore's casuistic definition of the word: 'that Irishmen were free in the same way as Englishmen, Scotsmen and Welshmen are free' and the motion was passed unanimously. However, when the results of the elections to the new Central Committee came through, and when Hyde saw how the new Committee would indeed be 'safe from the IRB viewpoint', he swept his papers from the table and left the hall. The following day he tendered this resignation from the League on health grounds.

Extraordinarily, the habit of loudly proclaiming the non-political aims of the League survived, even after it was completely, and obviously, dominated by radical nationalists. In 1918, Hyde wrote a private account of this phenomenon:

> ... I heard him [Seán T Ó Ceallaigh] myself speak to a crowded meeting in the Mansion House saying he spoke as a representative of Sinn Féin - he, the secretary of the Gaelic League. Notwithstanding this, a number of Sinn Féiners make it a point to set up a terrible hullabaloo if anyone ventures to say that the Gaelic League is political. This is part of that obliquity of vision, amounting almost to a disease, a kink of the mind, which I have observed in numerous representatives of that party. The fact, however, remains that they have left the Gaelic League a body to which no Redmondite and no Unionist can any longer subscribe *(ibid,* 73).

The 1915 meeting was the moment when the language movement was subsumed into the nationalist political movement. From the start, as I have noted, the League was ambivalent in its attitude to Irish nationalism. Although Hyde attempted to create an ethos which could create a space for non-nationalists, that effort itself was ambivalent, and ultimately failed. I can trace no unionists involved with the language who were not already involved before the first few years of the century. The importance of the 1915 *Ard-Fheis* was that it linked the Gaelic League unambiguously not only with nationalism, but with one section within the broader nationalist movement, that it became no more than the cultural wing of a political, and ultimately military, movement, and that its place within that movement was subordinate.

It may be useful to examine both the advantages and disadvantages for the language of the League's engagement with nationalist politics. In the first place, it is more than possible that the League would never have had the impact on Irish society which it did have without the driving force of nationalism, and that it would have been as squeaky-clean and ineffectual as its predecessors, the Gaelic Union and the Society for the Preservation of the Irish Language.

In addition, within a very few years, the group which instigated the takeover of the League in 1915 came to dominate the politics of the newly independent Irish Free State. The revival of Irish was a major ideological plank in the policies of both pro-treaty and anti-treaty post-independence parties. There was, in fact, sharp competition between them to be identified as the party which could be seen to be doing most for the language revival.

On the other hand, some of those involved in committing the League to a narrowly political programme later regretted their actions. Even Eoin Mac Néill, who succeeded Hyde as President of the League, and, as Minister of Education, became responsible for much of the early state revival policies, later wrote: 'I now think that the Gaelic League ... should have kept entirely clear of politics, and that its failure to do so, for which I am in part responsible, has been bad for the objects of the

League ...' (Ó Huallacháin 1991, 115). Obviously, Mac Néill's interpretation should be read in terms of the third, narrower form of politics I have tried to define above.

Among the disadvantages of the politicisation of the League was an almost complete polarisation of unionist and nationalist perspectives on the language. The political subtext of the League's early ideology may have raised unionist suspicions, and its increasing identification with radical nationalism in the years between the Home Rule crisis and partition confirmed them. This partly explains, even if it does not excuse, the brutality of the Ulster Unionist Party's treatment of the language in the Northern Ireland state.

However, a surprisingly large minority of northern unionists today show an interest in the language. Although some of this may stem from a fascination with the otherness of what is seen as a unified Gaelic/Catholic/nationalist package, it is also rooted in the crisis of identity which is now affecting unionism. Some of those who are seeking for a more satisfactory sense of identity than a denial of Irishness are beginning to look towards the nineteenth century, when it was both possible and fashionable for unionists to be interested in the language.

The perception that the Irish language movement - if not necessarily the language itself - is closely identified with nationalism remains a barrier to these people. This identification, it must be said, is based on past and current realities. That it is a current reality is clear from a recent article by Gearóid Ó Caireallán, Hyde's successor as the President of the Gaelic League, entitled *'An Ghaeilge sna Sé Chontae'* [Irish in the Six Counties]. Ó Caireallán's priority is the development of a 'vigorous, living' language community. He argues that unionists in Northern Ireland will see any developments in favour of Irish as 'concessions to nationalists'. Nationalist political parties, he argues, have no genuine commitment to the language, and his concern in this article is to secure a prominent place for Irish on their agenda so that the language will benefit from horse-trading between nationalist and unionist parties.

It could be argued that this approach is purely pragmatic: that in the reductive world of Northern Ireland, where all issues become the constitutional issue, the only way to find support for Irish is by promoting the language through those who cannot refuse to be supportive. This would be done in the regretful knowledge that, as happened with Hyde, such an approach would link the language ever more firmly with nationalism, and make a mockery of the movement's continuing claims to be non-political. The passage quoted below, however, suggests that the author did not have to wrestle too hard with his conscience in choosing this route. It also illustrates that old habits die hard, for the passage does contain a pale reflection of Hyde's genuine non-sectarian and ambivalent non-political approach, linked with some incoherent gestures towards the rhetoric of common heritage:

> And on the other side of the story, there is the British government.
>
> This is the crowd that has been tormenting Irish speakers throughout this country for hundreds of years. They did not do anything for Irish throughout the long years when they controlled all Ireland, and they continued with that anti-policy [sic] during their time in the Six Counties.
>
> Whatever concessions northern Irish-speakers got in recent years, they were hard won from the authorities.
>
> Let it not be forgotten that there were native speakers of Irish alive in the area of the Six Counties when the northern state was founded.
>
> There were speakers in County Tyrone, in County Antrim and in County Down.
>
> Stormont never did anything to preserve or conserve that native learning. Ethnic cleansing was the only policy the Unionists adopted and except for the Irish Folklore Commission in Dublin, we would not have even the archaeological [sic] remains.
>
> But things have changed and we may be on the threshold of a new era. We'll see.
>
> Irish fits naturally and comfortably into the framework of

parity of esteem, that is to say that the Irish language aspect of northern life must be promoted - brought up to speed, so to speak -if nationalists and Catholics are to be satisfied.

Without doubt, Irish has a cross-community aspect. There is evidence that certain Protestants are taking an interest in the language today - as they always did - and I welcome that.

But the development of Irish should not be dependent on Protestants taking an interest in it. And it cannot be said that Irish should be promoted only on a cross-community basis.

There is nothing in Irish to prevent Protestants, unionists and loyalists from taking an interest in it, just as they can take an interest in football, hurling, camogie, traditional music and Irish dancing if they wish to.

But if they do not wish to, that is up to them. There is no harm in trying to attract them, and it is necessary not to put any obstacles in their way.

But it must be admitted that the Irish language is a basic, inseparable part of Irish culture and any group which takes on Irish is taking on Irishness (Ó Cairealláin 1997, 5).

Now that the language movement appears set for a period of intense politicisation, where is the space for those of us engaged with the language and genuinely committed to making it available to the entire community? Irish is so weak in the unionist community in Northern Ireland that unionists cannot engage with the language without the help of (mainly nationalist) Irish-speakers. There is no point in engaging in denial, or playing the game which Hyde condemned - and of which he himself was to an extent guilty: 'that obliquity of vision, amounting almost to a disease, a kink of the mind', the tendency to claim that the language movement is non-political, while at the same time pursuing what is really a political agenda. This will not be believed. Nor is there any point in trying to use Irish culture, or arguments for adopting an Irish cultural identity to sugar the pill of Irish nationalism. Political antennae in Northern Ireland are too acute. On the other hand, cries to 'depoliticise'the language are usually disguised (political) attacks on nationalism, and a nationalist perspective on the language is just as valid as a unionist one.

It would be foolish to underestimate the difficulties of creating a neutral space for the language in our ideology-ridden society and it is unrealistic to expect that the entire Irish-language movement will break the mould which has now been established for the best part of a century. The challenge facing the Irish-speaking community is whether or not enough people can be found within it with the generosity, the courage, and the restraint to allow those of the unionist tradition to engage in the language on their own terms, as unionists. I believe, however, that there are enough Irish-speakers with that breadth of vision which would make such a development possible, and that there are enough unionists with a similar generosity of spirit to make it meaningful.

References

Blaney 1991
Roger Blaney, 'Gaels of North Lead Revival', Irish Language Supplement, *Irish News*, 21/11/1991, 38 - 41.

Breathnach, Ní Mhurchú 1990
Diarmuid Breathnach, Máire Ní Mhurchú, *Beathaisnéis a Dó*, an Clóchomhar, Dublin.

Census 1992
The Northern Ireland Census 1991, HMSO, Belfast, 1992.

Hyde 1894
Douglas Hyde, 'The Importance of De-Anglicising Ireland', in Charles Gavan Duffy, (ed) *The Revival of Irish Literature*.

Hyde 1901
Douglas Hyde, *A Literary History of Ireland*, London.

Hyde 1931
Dubhghlas de hÍde, *Mise agus an Connradh*, Oifig Dhíolta Foillsiúchán Rialtais, Dublin (1935 edition).

Ó Huallacháin 1991
Colmán Ó Huallacháin, *The Irish Language in Society*, Coleraine.

Ó Huallacháin 1994
Colmán Ó Huallacháin, *The Irish and Irish - a sociolinguistic analysis of the relationship between a people and their language*, Dublin.

The very dogs in Belfast will bark in Irish
The Unionist Government and the Irish language 1921-43
LIAM ANDREWS

In the late summer of 1920 the Ulster Unionist leadership drew up what amounted to a blueprint for the survival of the new Northern Ireland state. It called for the preferential treatment of the Protestant majority, the repression of rebels, and the employment of government supporters only in the public and security services.

> ... the steps now taken should be in accordance with the views of that majority. It should not be a Government in which both sides are treated as being equally entitled to a voice in whatever measures are taken ... The essential point to remember is that the Unionists hold that no rebel who wishes to set up a Republic can be regarded merely as a 'political opponent' but must be repressed ... The new Government officials and all new appointments to the Constabulary etc. should all be those who are prepared to accept this new form of Government.[1]

Around the same time Sir James Craig expressed concern to the British cabinet about the spread of rebel influences in Ulster and called for urgent help before loyalists took the law into their own hands.

> The Loyalist rank and file have determined to take action ... The Loyalist leaders ... find that their less restrained followers will not listen to them... They now feel that the situation is becoming so desperate that unless the [British] Government will take immediate action, it may be advisable for them to see what steps can be taken towards a system of <u>organised</u> reprisals against the rebels ... Ulster Loyalists implore the Government to take steps which will prove convincingly, not only that the Government is in earnest in preventing the coercion of the six

Counties of Ulster, but that it intends to distinguish between loyal subjects of His Majesty and those who are in active rebellion.[2]

The essential dynamic of the new state, with its future preoccupations, had already surfaced. The pragmatic element in the Unionist leadership would have to work out an accommodation with loyalism while maintaining friendly relationships with London. At the same time the criteria for the survival of the new state would have to be managed effectively. It was already obvious that there was no particular plan to involve the Catholic population in developments.

This was understandable. Both pragmatic unionists and their loyalist allies had inherited a similar value-system which identified rebels as the Catholic Irish.[3] However the pragmatists did not consider all Catholics as equally dangerous and realised that British tolerance would ultimately limit whatever strategies the new state might adopt to deal with them. Consequently they saw the need for a modicum of conciliation, where possible, to ensure the survival of the new state.[4]

Loyalists were not so restrained or discriminating. Their world-view, based on an extreme politicisation of British Protestantism, identified Catholicism as a powerful international conspiracy bent on the destruction of the British State.[5] Their deep-seated fear of Catholicism, exacerbated by the growth of Sinn Féin in Ulster and the violent activities of the Irish Republican Army (IRA), heightened their apprehension, particularly when Orange orators such as William Coote MP told them to prepare for a doomsday confrontation with the forces of Rome.[6] Little else was needed to act as catalyst for the mass intimidation of Catholic nationalists from their homes and employment by loyalists during the summer of 1920.[7]

By early September it was already clear to the pragmatists that their leadership credibility was in question unless loyalists could be restrained. Within days Craig had used this argument effectively to wrest vital concessions from the British cabinet. He gained a measure of local autonomy in security matters and permission to establish a special constabulary. The Ulster

Special Constabulary (USC), recruited mainly from the reconstituted Ulster Volunteer Force (UVF), allowed the Unionist leadership to exercise some authority over its militant supporters (and when a Northern Ireland police force, the Royal Ulster Constabulary [RUC], was later created, it too had a loyalist core). Nationalists saw the USC as an armed loyalist militia.[8]

If the political power of loyalism was such that it could be used effectively to influence British security policy at this early stage, it was bound to have a major impact on the policies of the new Northern Ireland government which was dependent on its support. This was borne out by the fact that Craig as Prime Minister was not only over-responsive to almost any non-Catholic pressure group[9] but had admitted on one occasion that whatever possible would be done to safeguard the loyalist interest.[10] Farrell goes so far as to suggest that in the relationship between the bourgeois pragmatists and their loyalist allies the former won the battle for the organisational control of unionism but the latter won the battle for political control.[11] That is not to say that the pragmatic element in the Unionist leadership was forced, in spite of itself, to accede to every loyalist whim. London could exert a moderating influence actively or passively depending on the nature of the issue and its distance from the central preoccupations of unionism.

A major unionist concern was to identify and suppress rebels and rebel influences. The corollary to this was a concern about loyalty, what constituted true loyalism and how it could be safeguarded. These considerations created limitless opportunities for individuals and ginger groups within the unionist community to act as vigilantes and moral policemen. Anything that seemed to weaken the unionist position or strengthen the enemy could be denounced as a betrayal. Such were unionist anxieties that denunciations like these could not be treated lightly. Against this background the new government of Northern Ireland had to formulate and implement policy on a range of controversial issues including the Irish language.

No accurate statistics exist relating to the numbers of Irish speakers in Ireland prior to 1851 when information on the language was first sought in the official census of population. Out of a total population of 6,552,386 in Ireland that year 1,524,286, or 23.3% spoke Irish. Allowing for a margin of error, an analysis of the figures according to birth dates reveals that Irish was already a minority language in Ireland among the age-group born before 1800.[12] The process of language shift from Irish to English continued until the end of the 19th century when the growth of cultural nationalism and the campaigning zeal of the newly established Gaelic League (1893) changed the climate of opinion throughout the country in favour of the language.

Prior to this the Irish language had had a romantic, academic and antiquarian appeal which transcended sectarian boundaries.[13] It had been the mother tongue of a number of small Protestant communities[14] and had also been used by a minority within the Protestant clergy as part of their missionary endeavour.[15] Beyond that most people saw the language as something of little value associated with the rural Catholic poor on the fringe of society.[16] However as Catholic political power grew in the course of the nineteenth century and Protestants began to seek sanctuary in a British Imperial identity,[17] the Irish language became increasingly associated with Catholicism.[18] This trend continued as the Catholic Church identified with Home Rule and became a powerful influence behind the Gaelic League.[19] The League sought to promote the revival of Irish as a spoken language on a non-political and non-sectarian basis and to appeal to all who had the best interests of Ireland at heart.[20]

The effects of language revivalism were to be seen in the Census returns of 1901 and 1911. Although the number of Irish speakers continued to decline in Gaeltacht (Irish speaking) areas, increases were recorded elsewhere in the country.[21] In 1851 the six counties of the historic province of Ulster which were later to become Northern Ireland had a number of small residual communities of native Irish speakers. The census revealed that 39,236 or 2.7% of the total population of the region spoke the language in that year.[22] The 1911 census indicated that the number of Irish speakers was now 28,729, or 2.3% of the total population.[23] This figure, which was influenced by the enthusiasm of revivalists, was probably an overestimate. It was however the same enthusiasm which created a new sense of identity amongst Irish speakers and revivalists alike, affecting the whole nationalist population.

Protestants, including members of the unionist community, were also active in the Gaelic League, particularly in the early stages, but they were a minority who could find its deference to Catholic values off-putting.[24] More typical of the unionist response to the organisation, perhaps, was a violent attack by loyalists on Gaelic League members in August 1905 as they returned home to Banbridge from the annual feis at Castlewellan.[25] There was already suspicion of the Gaelic League in unionist circles. Three months earlier the *Irish Weekly* reported that the Gaelic League, which was under police investigation for subversion, was considered by some loyalists to be a menace to the Empire.[26]

Even unionists with some regard for the study of Irish had reservations. In 1909 the Senate and Academic Council of the newly constituted Queen's University of Belfast, predominantly Protestant in religion and Unionist in politics, acceded to public pressure, spearheaded by the Gaelic League, in favour of establishing a lecturership in Celtic there, but that was as far as the University was prepared to go. Two years later, when an attempt was made to persuade the Senate to raise the lecturership to the status of a Chair, it was resisted, even though a deputation from a public meeting offered the University £1,000 in cash towards the cost. Moody and Beckett, in their official history of Queen's University, make the point that a similar offer on behalf of some other subject would have been more sympathetically received.[27]

Although the Gaelic League may have had little impact on

the world of unionism, it added a new dimension to the lives of nationalists in social, educational and political terms. Socially its branches, which were mostly in nationalist areas, provided a focus for the development of cultural and leisure activities for speakers and learners of Irish.[28] Locally and regionally the calendar was filled with Irish-Ireland indoor and outdoor entertainments with evocative titles like *aeridheacht, sgoraidheacht, seanchas, seilg, pléaráca, céilidhe, ceolchuirm* and *feis*. Gaelic League branches also offered localities unique educational opportunities. They provided courses in Irish for learners at different levels, taught them Irish songs and dances and held lectures on Irish history and folklore. They also encouraged local industrial enterprise and community solidarity based on an Irish-Ireland identity. Politically the Gaelic League lobbied for the recognition of the rights of Irish speakers and a higher status for the language in the public domain. A major success was the campaign to promote the teaching of Irish in the education system.[29] It was built on the achievements of the Society for the Preservation of the Irish Language which had managed in the late 1870s to persuade the authorities to allow the subject to be taught in national and intermediate schools.[30]

By 1921, due largely to pressure from the Gaelic League, the British Government had given the language a more privileged position than other optional and extra subjects on the fringes of the national school curriculum. Irish was available as an optional subject in all standards during the normal school day and as an extra fee-paying subject outside normal school hours from Standard III upwards. Teaching through the medium of Irish was permissible in national schools in areas where sufficient Irish was spoken locally. There were 'Irish speaking' areas in Co. Tyrone, but according to the Ministry of Education for Northern Ireland, these were not classified as bilingual districts.[31] Irish was taught as a subject for examination in secondary schools and for degree courses at universities. It was also available as an option in teacher-training colleges for prospective national teachers who sought teaching qualifications in Irish. Apart from that, the government supported the language by paying teacher training grants to independent Irish language colleges run by the Gaelic League and by validating their teacher training certificates. (There were two of these in Belfast, *Coláiste Chomhghaill* and *Ardsgoil Ultach*). Additional curriculum support was provided by the employment of a number of Irish Language Organisers who, with the inspectorate, helped to improve standards in the teaching of Irish in national schools.[32] Irish, in the years leading up to partition, had risen from relative obscurity to become an increasingly popular subject in the education system but its development had yet to reach maturity in terms of institutional support, teacher supply and the availability of suitable teaching materials.

Although no precise information is available concerning the number of schoolteachers who were qualified to teach Irish in Northern Ireland in the early 1920s or the number of schools involved, a good estimate can be made from educational statistics. At most there were perhaps 380 teachers, with basic qualifications in Irish, teaching the subject in 177 public elementary schools (as the national schools were now known). That amounted to approximately 24% of teachers in public elementary schools under Catholic management or 8% of the total elementary schoolteacher population in Northern Ireland.[33] There is a reference in Ministry files to 271 teachers teaching Irish in 191 schools during the period up to 1927.[34] It does not however include the number of qualified teachers who had no opportunity to teach the subject. School examination statistics suggest that all 24 secondary schools under Catholic management, that is approximately 31% of the total in Northern Ireland, had at least one teacher of Irish. Modern Irish was offered as part of the degree course in Celtic Studies at Queen's University and as an optional subject at St Mary's Training College.

As long as the Gaelic League's lobbying activities on behalf of Irish in education did not include an element of compulsion, there was no direct threat to the British imperial identity of unionists. There were however other areas where such a threat might have been more apparent. In lobbying for the equal treatment of Irish in any of the public services that affected the whole community, the Gaelic League presented unionists with a challenge. Depending on the nature of the challenge, unionists might see it not so much as a plea for equality as a calculated attempt to undermine their identity. If some loyalists were already hostile to the League in 1905 at a time when it was campaigning for recognition by the Post Office and the legal system of names and addresses in Irish, how much stronger would their antipathy be to this kind of activity in the aftermath of the 1916 rebellion when the League's association with sedition in the government's view caused it to be proclaimed.[35] If anything, this new status confirmed unionist suspicions that the organisation was part of an anti-British counter-culture dominated by Republican separatists and that its promotion of the Irish language might be nothing more than the promotion of sedition and disloyalty under another name.

Thus when the new northern state was established, unionists were aware of the Irish language and its importance to the nationalist community. It had its place in the education system and in the academic world; it had the support of the Catholic church; and in the political sphere it had close associations with the implacable enemy of unionism - republicanism. Its political and religious affiliations made it at best an object of suspicion and at worst an alien threat. Loyalists tended towards the latter viewpoint.

The Government of Ireland Act (1920) which partitioned Ireland had no built-in guarantees that the basic human rights of northern nationalists would be respected. It did however legislate against the state endowment of any religious denomination.[36] It was not so much the legislation as events on the ground that shaped Catholic nationalist attitudes towards the new state. The indiscriminate violence of loyalists against

Catholics during the early years of the state's formation, the continuous bias of the government and the legal system against them and the general climate of political uncertainty made most of them reluctant to recognise the authority of the northern state until they had no other alternative. Their loyalty was therefore in question from the beginning.

Meanwhile the first government of Northern Ireland installed in June 1921 began to give legislative force to the political and cultural priorities of unionism. The immediate concern was to eliminate republicanism as a military and political force and diminish the power and influence of Irish nationalism. Behind both of these political persuasions unionists, and particularly loyalists, saw the hidden hand of Rome whose disloyal influence over the Catholic population, they believed, was maintained through the pulpit, the confessional and Catholic schools. Judging by the public utterances of unionist politicians, it looked as though Catholic Church interests too might be targeted.[37] Measures to reinforce loyalty were also under consideration. What took shape in Northern Ireland within a few years was a political system based on the British parliamentary model but embedded in a framework of repressive conservative reaction.

The most powerful and effective legislative weapon to be used against nationalists in general and republicans in particular was the Civil Authorities (Special Powers) Act of 1922 which gave the government a wide range of draconian powers including exclusion, internment without trial and the banning of organisations, literature, meetings and processions.[38] The Ministry of Home Affairs, headed by Dawson Bates (an uncompromising loyalist) and supported by the RUC and USC, used these powers to neutralise the IRA and drive republicans underground in disarray. The Local Government Act of the same year undermined the political power of nationalists by gerrymandering local council areas in favour of unionists and abolishing PR in local council elections. The legislation also imposed an oath of allegiance on all local authority officials.

The following year an oblique attack was launched on Catholic education. The Londonderry Education Act (1923) created new schemes of school management which penalised Catholic schools financially. Shortly afterwards schoolteachers were obliged to take an oath of allegiance.[39] Discrimination against Catholics became accepted unionist practice in employment and the administration of justice, and the manipulation of the franchise in the interests of unionist domination continued.[40] As these developments took place a policy towards the Irish language emerged.

Surprisingly, the Ministry of Home Affairs had little to do with it. The Gaelic League was not listed amongst the banned organisations and Irish language material seized in police raids on republican suspects was invariably returned as being harmless. Officials in the Ministry or the prison service might object to internees such as Charles Mawhinney having access to study material in Irish but by and large there was no blanket prohibition.[41] Perhaps the consensus was that subversives might be interested in Irish but that they did not actually use it for any subversive purpose. If unionists believed that the language was essential to the building of a subversive mentality, their anxieties might centre more on the activities of the Ministry of Education than those of any other government department. This Ministry was in fact the focus of the attack on the Irish language which began in December 1921.

In parliament William Grant, an ex-UVF organiser and future cabinet minister, was first to raise the issue during a debate on the Education Estimates.

> I want to know if the Minister of Education considers it advisable to make provision for an Organiser of Irish Languge Instruction under this House, because the people who are in favour of that particular language do not take up their seats in this House, and I think during their absence we ought not to make any provision for that particular matter.

He was immediately supported by Thompson Donald who

exclaimed,

> I agree with my hon. Friend. There is no need for one Organiser of Irish Language Instruction. What do we want with the Irish language here? There is no need for it at all. [42]

No Nationalist members were present to hear these sentiments. They were already boycotting the new parliament.

On 1 February 1922, under the partition arrangements, control of the educational services relating to Northern Ireland was transferred from Dublin to Belfast. Two days later the northern Minister of Education, Lord Londonderry, made an important public statement on the status of Irish under his administration. He said that due regard should be given to the special characteristics of Northern Ireland. In relation to Irish it meant that it would remain as an optional subject in the curriculum as long as pupils wanted it and teachers were available to teach it. Beyond that he was not prepared to go.

> ...let me say at once that I would not be prepared to countenance any proposal containing, directly or indirectly, any element of compulsion on, or undue preference to pupils or teachers in regard to instruction in Irish.

In regard to a proposal from the Dublin-based Intermediate Board that examinations in subjects other than Irish might be answered in Irish he said,

> ... as your Minister of Education, I will not for one moment allow the use of the so-called Irish language in the Intermediate examinations for Northern Ireland in the answers to any papers except those set upon the Irish language as the subject of examinations. [43]

As far as he was concerned, the Irish language was to have no existence beyond the confines of its own subject area.

His remarks further alienated the beleaguered Catholic nationalist community and gave an added incentive to a growing number of Catholic teachers and school managers who had decided to launch a non-recognition campaign against the northern Ministry with financial support from the Provisional Government in Dublin. Their aim (which was part of a broader plan) was to destabilise the newly transferred educational services in order to force the northern government to come to terms with the South or make concessions. Their justification was the treatment of the Catholic community by the northern government and its armed supporters and the anti-Catholic and anti-Irish sentiments of prominent unionists.[44] One concession sought by a senior clerical supporter of the campaign was the right of Catholic schools in the north to adopt the programme and timetable of southern Ireland.[45] Michael Collins, head of the Provisional Government, blamed Londonderry's attitude towards Irish for the breakdown in relationships between the education ministries of both states.[46]

The campaign lasted ten months and involved approximately 700 teachers, including at least one third of elementary schools under Catholic management. All the Catholic secondary schools boycotted the Ministry's public examinations that year. In the midst of the campaign R. J. McKeown, the Parliamentary Secretary to the Minister of Education, announced to cries of approval in the northern parliament that the post of Organiser of Irish Language Instruction had been abolished.[47]

On 10 August 1922 the Ministry began to lay the groundwork for other policy decisions affecting Irish in elementary education. The Senior Chief Inspector was asked to consider a range of questions in joint conference with the Irish inspector and another colleague and to draw up a report for the Minister's guidance. Topics included how much time should be devoted to the teaching of Irish per week during ordinary school hours; should other compulsory subjects be dropped in whole or in part to accommodate Irish; should Irish be taught as an ordinary and an extra subject in parallel using the same or extended programmes; and should the teaching of Irish be forbidden where teachers were not qualified.[48]

On the same day Bonaparte Wyse, the Assistant Secretary, drafted policy recommendations in relation to independent Irish language colleges. These were accepted by Lewis McQuibban, the Permanent Secretary, five days later. It was agreed that the Ministry should no longer recognise or fund any of these colleges in Northern Ireland; that teachers would still be allowed extra vacation to attend them and perhaps others close to the border on the southern side, but that their certificates would be no longer recognised; instead the Ministry would award its own on the basis of an oral and written examination.[49]

Meanwhile pressure was mounting on all those involved in the non-recognition campaign to end it. On 5 August the Ministry sent letters to the managers of vested schools involved in the campaign threatening them with legal action and from 19 August onwards the Provisional Government could see the financial necessity for disengagement.[50]

Before any other policy changes could be made affecting the Irish language, negotiations began to resolve the teachers' non-recognition campaign. Fr Macaulay and Dr Hendley, representing the interests of Catholic school managers, opened contact with McQuibban and John Harbison, an executive committee member of the Irish National Teachers' Organisation (INTO) met him. Harbison, acting in a personal capacity, asked for information that might help bring the campaign to an end.[51] Two of the three issues he raised dealt with the Irish language. He wanted to know if the Ministry would recognise an alternative programme that would allow Irish to be taught during normal school hours as part of the ordinary school curriculum, and if the Ministry would establish centres in Northern Ireland where elementary schoolteachers could learn Irish during school holidays.[52] It was clear at this point that those leading the campaign believed that the Ministry intended to remove Irish completely from the curriculum during the normal school day and deprive elementary schoolteachers of the facilities to become qualified teachers of Irish.

McQuibban responded by saying that he could give no pledge as to what the Ministry would do but suggested that the claim for an alternative programme for northern schools would be greatly strengthened if a similar concession was made in the south which would allow the Protestant minority to forgo compulsory Irish. He also pointed out that there were several officially recognised Irish language colleges in Northern Ireland where elementary schoolteachers could study Irish during vacation time. He failed to mention the fact that he was recently party to a decision not to fund or recognise these colleges or their certificates any longer. He concluded by saying that there was every disposition to treat the teachers concerned sympathetically so far as this could be done without sacrifice of principle or without acting in a way that would be unlikely to meet with the approval of parliament.[53]

On 7 September McQuibban met Macaulay and Hendley who promised to help bring the non-recognition campaign to an end.[54] The following day H. G. Garrett, the Senior Chief Inspector, and W. H. Welply submitted their report on the teaching of Irish. They recommended that it should be taught for no more than an hour and a half per week as an optional subject within ordinary school hours; that history might be dropped in its favour; that the Inspector of Irish Instruction should furnish statements concerning the efficiency of teaching in schools where Irish was being offered in order to assist other inspectors in connection with their general reports; that Irish could also be taught for at least 40 hours per annum as an extra subject for fees; that in schools where Irish was being taught as an optional and extra subject in parallel the same programme should be used, but that a higher standard would be required than in a school where Irish was taught as an extra only; and that teachers without paper qualifications might teach Irish provided that they obtained the necessary qualifications within a year. No action was taken because a general settlement of the non-recognition campaign was expected soon.[55]

Meanwhile Macaulay and Hendley had already provided

McQuibban with an outline of the campaigners' negotiating position. It included a call for Irish to be taught for half an hour a day by competent teachers in schools where parents were agreeable and for the inclusion of books with an 'Irish-Ireland' outlook on the Ministry's list of recommended texts.[56]

McQuibban then briefed Londonderry. He was very sympathetic towards the Catholic school authorities who, in spite of very difficult circumstances, had managed to conduct two thirds of their schools in accordance with the Ministry's regulations. He argued that the Ministry's administrative record so far had proved that there were no grounds for the belief which may have been sincerely held that the government would interfere with teachers' ideals as Catholics and Irishmen. He therefore felt that the demand for concessions in regard to the teaching of Irish and the use of books with an Irish-Ireland outlook was something in the nature of an attempt at political justification for past action, which would also encourage support from the south. He consequently recommended that the Minister should not negotiate on this issue 'with a small minority of teachers as a condition of their readmission to relationship with the Ministry'. He believed that the Ministry's regulations governing the modification of school timetables which appeared in March was an adequate mechanism for dealing with the matter.[57] He was mistaken. The campaign dragged on.

On 11 November 1922 Wyse gave McQuibban Garrett and Welply's report on the teaching of Irish. He said that he agreed with its recommendations but had not submitted it earlier because a resolution of the non-recognition campaign looked likely. Now however he reported that schools were introducing Irish into the timetable in excess of these recommendations.[58] In the interval the Provisional Government had decided not to support the teachers' non-recognition campaign financially beyond October.[59]

According to John Duffin, the chief organiser of the campaign in the north, the last stumbling block to a settlement was Londonderry's opposition to concessions on the teaching of Irish. This may be true, but it is also possible that, following McQuibban's advice, Londonderry was really opposed in principle to something else — giving legitimacy to the grievances of 'a small minority of teachers' by having any negotiations at all with them. Ultimately the deadlock was broken when Londonderry and one of his officials met two of the teachers' representatives, Duffin and Peter McGivern, and it was agreed that if history became an optional rather than a required subject enough time could be found for the teaching of Irish during the normal school day.[60] The fact that this course of action had already been recommended by officials as early as 8 September 1922 suggests that Londonderry's real concession was the meeting itself.

On 22 November McQuibban drew up a four-page memorandum on Irish for Londonderry which listed the main recommendations of the September report and provided some background information. It stated that there were no bilingual districts in Northern Ireland; that Irish might be taught as an optional subject within school hours in all standards and as an extra subject outside ordinary school hours in third and higher standards. McQuibban agreed with the recommendation to drop history in favour of Irish because 'the kind of history that would be taught in schools where it is desired to foster the study of Irish would be likely to have a bias of a very undesirable nature'. He was also of the view that the optional study for those who did not want to learn Irish 'must be definitely and clearly stated in the time-table'. Londonderry signed his approval six days later.[61] By the end of the month the teachers' non-recognition campaign was over.[62]

St Mary's, initially the only teacher training college in Northern Ireland, was under Catholic management and had also been involved in the non-recognition campaign. It would not accept candidates from Northern Ireland nominated by the Ministry of Education but looked south for support. However changes in the curriculum of training colleges which accepted

Dublin's leadership were rejected by the northern Ministry. Therefore St Mary's was in danger of losing its status as a teacher training college in Northern Ireland unless it came to terms with the new government. An agreement was reached between both parties in 1923 which brought the college under the jurisdiction of the Ministry.[63] The teaching of Irish as an optional subject was not affected. The value of Irish in the College however was already being undermined by policy changes affecting the teaching of Irish in schools.

By April 1923 a number of important decisions had been made, some of which were published in Circular P.21. The post of Organiser of Irish Instruction had been abolished; the existence of English-Irish bilingualism in Northern Ireland had been dismissed; the teaching of Irish as an optional subject had been reduced to 90 minutes a week in public elementary schools; and recognition and funding had been withdrawn from independent Irish language colleges.

Not every unionist was pleased. In parliament Sir Robert Lynn, the hardline Unionist chairman of the Ministry's important Departmental Committee on the Educational Services, wanted to know if the Ministry still intended to retain the services of an Organiser of Irish Instruction and whether a circular had been issued which allowed history to be dropped in favour of Irish. 'I respectfully suggest to the Ministry of Education that history - that is, real history, not imaginative history of the Irish type - would be of more benefit to the schools than the teaching of Irish. That is a purely sentimental thing. None of these people who take up Irish ever know anything about it. They can spell their own names badly in Irish, but that is all. I do not think it is worth spending any money on'. In reply McKeown said that he could assure members that there was now no such thing as an organiser of Irish language and that no undue preference would be given to Irish history.[64]

At this point two important educational projects were nearing completion - the final report of the Ministry's

Departmental Committee under Lynn's chairmanship and the passing of Londonderry's Education Bill which would shape the future of education in Northern Ireland. In both instances unionists voiced concerns about loyalty. During the debate on the Education Bill H. S. Morrison, an MP for Queen's University, proposed an amendment that would enable the Ministry to assist, at the request of education authorities, in educating children in the principles of loyalty to the Empire, good citizenship and respect for their country's flag. He did not propose to force the popular opinion of Ulster on anybody but said,

> ... while I think force is unnecessary, I think it is very necessary that we in Ulster now should insist on Ulster ideals prevailing. We think ... that this Empire of ours is the greatest instrument that God has yet created for liberty and progress and humanity ... we want to teach the coming generation that it is our greatest possession.

He praised the honesty of the English Diehards and accused some Northern Ireland Government ministers of half-heartedness. He was immediately supported by Lynn who claimed that the Ministry was as anxious as anybody could possibly be to see that loyalty was taught in schools. Mrs Dehra Chichester (later Parker), another hardline unionist and future Parliamentary Secretary to the Minister of Education, then rose to her feet calling for the teaching of civics, loyalty and respect for the flag to be made obligatory. Replying for the Ministry, McKeown said that this was scarcely the proper place for the amendment, but he assured Members that it was the Ministry's desire to turn out good citizens. In fact, he maintained that the Ministry would go very much further than the amendment and see to it that education authorities would comply and concluded by saying,

> The one thing the Ministry has in mind is to turn out good and loyal citizens - citizens who will respect the flag. That is the intention of the Ministry and we would not be faithful to our

principles if we did not do it.

The amendment was withdrawn.[65]

When the final report of the Lynn Committee appeared shortly afterwards it, too, placed great emphasis on loyalty. It recommended that no aid be given to any school in which principles subversive of the authority of the state were inculcated; that no books should be read to which reasonable objections might be entertained on political grounds; that all teachers should, as a condition of their recognition, be required to give an undertaking to carry out faithfully the regulations of the Ministry; and that the Ministry of Education should encourage in all state-aided schools the flying of the Union Jack on suitable occasions.[66]

There was an implicit threat in all of these recommendations directed at the cultural values and politics of nationalists which, if enforced by vigilant loyalists, could effectively censor even the most innocuous teaching material. The unionist community was never short of such people, as subsequent history shows. The threat was real. The Ministry subsequently censored all textbooks used in connection with history, citizenship, economics and Irish and supplied schools with lists of approved books in these subjects.

The Report attacked the Irish language, claiming that it was receiving preferential treatment. It called for the abolition of fees for Irish as an extra subject below fifth standard and all other privileges, for which it claimed there was no justification, and recommended that the language be treated in the same manner as Latin and French. Here the Committee laid down policy guidelines for the treatment of Irish which were adopted by the Ministry and have been effective until recently - that Irish had the same status in the curriculum as a dead or foreign language and merited no preferential treatment.[67]

In spite of the Report's robust approach to loyalty and its negative attitude towards Irish it did not please all the Committee members. Two broke ranks to express even more extreme views in a reservation to the main text. One was Dehra Chichester and the other William Miller, a senior Orangeman. On loyalty they remarked,

> The curse of this country has been the seditious teaching which its children have been so long receiving and loyalty to their mother country has never been systematically brought to them. If it is considered expedient and necessary to fly the flag of state from the schools of Canada and the United States, is it not even more necessary to do so in Northern Ireland? In our opinion not only should the flag be flown over every state aided school but the youngest children should be assembled at very frequent intervals and taught to salute the flag, thus inculcating loyalty in the children.[68]

When it came to Irish their hostility was palpable.

> There is one recommendation of the Committee which we very strongly protest against. We have no objection to anyone who wishes to learn the Irish language, but we must strongly object to the minds and brains of our children being burdened with such useless work; and we have still stronger objection to the teaching of that language being paid out of the public purse. If parents wish their children to learn Irish or any other useless language they should pay for it out of their own pockets, but it should not be a charge upon either tax or rate payers.[69]

The Ministry had its first opportunity to put the Lynn Committee strategy against Irish into operation the following year when it produced its first programme of instruction for public elementary schools. The teaching of Irish as an optional subject was prohibited below Standard V. Optional subjects were then divided into two groups, A and B, with Irish in the latter along with French, Latin, algebra and geometry. The Ministry stipulated that at least two optional subjects should be taken from group A, which contained history, science, nature study and horticulture, before group B could be considered.[70] At best, Irish could only be a third choice and in such a crowded programme it would be lucky to be taught at all. During the consultation process the INTO called for the retention of Irish as an optional subject in all standards as before, but this was rejected by the Ministry.[71] The new regulations affecting Irish appeared when the new programme was published in June 1924.

It immediately became difficult to study Irish in public elementary schools during the normal school day and below Standard V it seemed impossible. As an optional subject the language now had the status which conformed to typical unionist thinking. It was classified amongst the foreign and dead languages, as far away from the core curriculum as possible, without actually being totally banned. The new strictures on Irish were offset a little by Circular P.21 which was still in force. It allowed Irish to be taught in place of history which, according to the new programme, remained an optional subject in Standards III and IV. This anomaly gave Irish language supporters an opportunity to press for improvements in the 1924 programme, which they did with some success. But the tide was against them. The number of schools that taught Irish as an optional subject dropped from at least 160 in the year 1924-5 to 78 in the year 1927-8, a fall of just over 50%.[72]

In spite of this there remained one area of the curriculum untouched by the new programme - the teaching of extra subjects for fees. It continued to offer an opening for an expansion in the teaching of Irish when other avenues had closed, but only from Standard III upwards. The Ministry was aware of this too. Its annual report for 1924-5 revealed a substantial increase in the funding of Irish as an extra subject following the introduction of the new programme.[73]

The Ministry now moved to curb this development. A proposal to impose a cut-back had been under consideration since August 1925 but action was postponed pending a report from the Salaries Council.[74] At an opportune moment a Unionist senator, William Barclay, attacked the government for wasting public money on the teaching of Irish as an extra subject. He claimed that it had no commercial value and argued that the

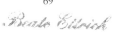

teaching of Irish was part of a long-term Republican plan to drive the English language and English speakers out of Ireland. He said that this was being attempted through a policy of compulsion in the Free State and by slipping the language into the schools of Northern Ireland. 'It is not right', he declared, 'that a man who is an Imperialist, or a Loyalist or a Constitutionalist should be taxed ... in support of the (sic) Irish Republican propaganda'. He concluded by asking the government for an answer that would help ease the minds of a great many loyalist subjects in Belfast.[75]

Barclay got his answer within days. On 11 May 1926 the Ministry introduced new regulations governing extra and special subjects in public elementary schools. Fees ceased to be paid for the teaching of Irish as an extra subject in Standards III and IV from that year onwards.[76] The result, according to the Ministry's annual Report for 1927-8, was a significant drop in the number of schools teaching Irish as an extra subject. In terms of pupil numbers it amounted to a a reduction of 70%.[77]

By late 1926 the Gaelic League in Northern Ireland had begun to rally under the leadership of *Comhaltas Uladh*, a new executive body within the organisation which now had special responsibility for branches in Ulster and Co. Louth.[78] It immediately opened up correspondence with the Ministry of Education and in February 1927 was represented in a strong deputation which met the new Minister of Education, Lord Charlemont, and three of his officials to discuss the teaching of Irish. The deputation, which was led by senior Catholic clergy, sought a restoration of the 1922 regulations affecting Irish in national schools but had to be content with two small concessions. Charlemont agreed to allow Irish to continue to be taught as an optional subject instead of history in Standards III and IV and to review the regulations affecting optional subject grouping, but he made it clear that as far as he was concerned French was more useful than Irish which in Northern Ireland was a dead or dying language.[79]

Although the meeting achieved next to nothing for the

Gaelic League, it later became an embarrassment to Charlemont in the run-up to the Orange celebrations of July. On 20 June John F. Charles, a columnist in the *Northern Whig*, attacked him for meeting the Gaelic League and promising to allow Irish to be taught in place of history. He described it as a very serious matter of no small political significance. He then warned readers of Gaelic League activities in the Free State. According to him, the League was responsible for having the street names changed to Irish, for having all mention of the British Empire obliterated from official documents and for having the King's head on postage stamps and postal orders disfigured by a heavy inscription in Irish. He claimed that the League also had undue influence in Irish political life and that it blacklisted parliamentary candidates who had not pledged themselves to Gaelicise parliament, public administration and education. In Charles' view it would be a serious error to allow a useless and unnecessary subject like Irish to be taught in schools, especially in place of history, and he urged the Minister to reconsider his action or explain fully his assurance to the Gaelic League. This he argued was a matter of great importance because it was merely the thin end of the wedge and would be used as a precedent for further overtures which would soon lead the government into a position similar to that of the southern parliament - being involved by a crowd of idealists in a ridiculous policy.[80]

Shortly afterwards, the Ministry received an angry letter from a Mr Wilson who purported to be the Master of an Orange Lodge. He attacked the Minister for meeting such a disloyal body as the Gaelic League and making a promise to them without consulting higher authority. The promise, he claimed, amounted to asking the loyal people of Ulster to pay for the teaching of Irish to rebels and he assured him that trouble would follow once parents, teachers and Protestants got wind of developments. 'We in the six counties won't have Irish and you can't force it on the people against their wish', he said and called on the Minister to rescind the decision. He then threatened to report the matter to every lodge in Belfast.[81]

Charlemont's immediate concern was to avoid trouble with the Orange Order. He wrote to Wilson Hungerford, secretary of the Ulster Unionist Council, briefing him on the teaching of Irish and asked him to do a little propaganda work for the Ministry in regard to Wilson's letter. He saw the advantage of clarifying the issue before the Twelfth of July celebrations and hoped that Hungerford might find someone who could approach Wilson personally and explain the real facts to him. He concluded by remarking that the position regarding the teaching of Irish remained unchanged despite the efforts of the deputation in question.[82]

Hungerford came up with a novel solution. He published a letter of his own on the teaching of Irish in the *Northern Whig* on 2 July under the pseudonym 'Truth'. He began by saying that he held no brief for the Gaelic League but felt that too much had been made of the meeting between the Minister of Education and a deputation from that organisation. He pointed out that any body of citizens were entitled to put their views before the government but that it was another matter whether the government would accede to their request. He deplored the influence exercised by the Gaelic League in Southern Ireland saying,

> No Protestant or Loyalist can defend the action of that League in imposing with tyrant hand the teaching of Irish on an unwilling and helpless people.

But this, he declared, was unlikely to happen in Northern Ireland because

> Lord Charlemont is a Minister of firmness and backbone and the members of the Gaelic League have found that he is neither to be cajoled nor threatened into doing something which would be subversive of the true educational interests of the Province.

Charlemont, he assured readers, had told the deputation that under no circumstances would there be any compulsion regarding the teaching and learning of Irish in public elementary schools and that they should be grateful to his lordship for his resolute attitude. He then explained that the teaching of Irish in public elementary schools was not an innovation but had been introduced into the curriculum as an optional subject by the old National Board and that consequently no change had taken place. Finally, he returned to the main point that there would never be any compulsion; that Irish could not be forced down the throats of Ulster Loyalists and that if parents permitted their children to be taught that useless language they had no-one to blame but themselves.[83]

Towards the end of the year a small *Comhaltas Uladh* deputation met Ministry officials again to clear up some doubtful points in the regulations regarding the teaching of Irish in public elementary schools.[84] The upshot was a decision by the Ministry to produce a new circular on the subject. In expressing his desire to have this done Wyse, the new Permanent Secretary, explained the Ministry's position to a colleague, 'In the drafting we should avoid carefully giving any impression that we desire to encourage the teaching of the language.' [85] The circular in question, P.133, was published in March 1928.

Incredibly this innocuous document in turn created problems for the government. On 9 June an extreme right-wing loyalist organisation, the Loyalty League, which had its base in London and at least one 'outpost' in Belfast, wrote to the Prime Minister from its Irish Headquarters to attack it.[86] The League's Belfast secretary, E. J. Clarke, condemned the Circular as unwise and very dangerous because he believed that it would in effect subsidise an anti-British and disloyal faction whose political and religious activities were subversive of Ulster Protestantism and all that it stood for. He continued,

> True Britishers have scarcely an academic interest in the Irish language and our Protestant brethern in the Irish Free State are finding it hard indeed to educate their children and place them, owing to the callous and cruel exactions of the Education

Authority, in imposing a worthless study of Gaelic on all children. As loyal subjects of his Majesty the King, we strongly resent this pandering to a cunning foe, for although presented in the form of an optional subject, it can soon be arranged that each school will require a Gaelic teacher, even in Protestant districts, and each teacher will as a rule be a secret fomenter of strife.

He concluded by urging the Prime Minister to defer the circular because a strong spirit of resentment against the government was growing rapidly in Belfast and provincial towns.[87]

Two days later the Cabinet Secretary, Charles Blackmore, asked the Ministry of Education for a full memorandum on the teaching of Irish in public elementary schools[88] and on the same day William Grant MP raised the concerns of the Loyalty League in a letter to J. H. Robb, Charlemont's Parliamentary Secretary.[89] Robb replied promptly telling Grant that there was nothing secretive about Circular P.133; that some 3,000 copies had been issued; that the Circular merely clarified the position in relation to the teaching of Irish; and that that actually involved a reduction in the opportunities for teaching the subject. He ended with these words,

> We found Irish teaching in being when we took over and so far from encouraging it, we have been reducing facilities, and as a result Irish is taught in only 149 schools as against 242 in 1922. I do not think that the Loyalty League would have felt any alarm if they had known the facts. [90]

The Ministry's memorandum to the Prime Minister was equally candid. It explained that the Ministry had had to decide in 1922 whether to withdraw all privileges relating to the teaching of Irish or to modify them.

> It was felt desirable on the one hand, to curtail opportunities for Irish teaching, but on the other hand, it was believed to be more politic to allow its continuance as an optional subject to a modified extent. It was clear that any proposal to prohibit it altogether would give certain parties an opportunity of raising a grievance and at the same time intensify the desire of a section of the people

to apply themselves to its study. It was decided to adopt a middle course and allow the teaching of Irish to continue with certain limitations.

The memorandum then listed the limitations resulting from changes to the regulations and commented that the general effect of these changes had been to diminish the number of schools and pupils studying Irish in Northern Ireland. In addition to the information already given to Grant, the memorandum mentioned that numbers studying Irish as an extra subject had fallen from 5,531 in 1923-4 to 1,290 in 1926-7 and that less than 25% of public elementary schools under Roman Catholic management now gave instruction in Irish.[91]

Wyse, the Permanent Secretary, sent Blackmore the memorandum on 20 June 1928 with the comment, 'I venture to say that our handling of the question has shown more wisdom than would have been apparent in a policy of strict repression.'[92] Six days later, Blackmore replied to the Loyalty League using a draft prepared by Wyse. It gave a brief history of the Ministry's efforts to restrict the teaching of Irish and ended by saying that since the tendency to study Irish was not increasing, there was little fear of any of those undesirable consequences which the League forsaw arising.[93]

The League was not convinced. Lord Craigavon received another letter from its Belfast secretary on the eve of the Twelfth of July celebrations. He expressed his committee's pleasure at the curtailment of facilities for the teaching of Irish but their irritation that any Ulster money was being spent at all on the subject. He was concerned about the Irish language movement which he claimed to be anti-British and anti-Protestant. He argued that most of the brains behind the 1916 rebellion were in this movement and continued,

> The fact that certificates are supplied by the Ulster Government to enable rebellious spirits to propagate sedition as an 'extra' subject is strongly resented by Loyalists. The language is of no practical utility, but may be of much value to incipient traitors, as a means

of fomenting trouble.

He accepted that in Belfast the language movement had originally been non-sectarian and had attracted all classes but claimed that Roman Catholic propaganda had soon forced Protestants to leave. He now appealed to Craigavon for unity in support of 'Ulster ideals' and the loyalist position and called on him to cancel Irish as an extra subject.[94]

Craigavon's reply, which was marked 'confidential' and signed by one of his officials, expressed sympathy with the League's concerns. However it continued,

> He [the Prime Minister] is by no means convinced that repressive measures would affect the object which both you and he desire. A prohibition of Irish teaching in the schools might have a result the very opposite to that intended. It would be proclaimed by interested parties as a provocative and arbitrary act on the part of the Government and would be used as a potent means of arousing in many people an interest in a study to which there is good reason to believe they are gradually and steadily becoming indifferent. In the view of the Government it is better to keep a control by means of regulations over activities of this character than to drive them underground where they will undoubtedly tend to germinate and exert a baneful influence ... You may rest assured that the Government is watching the situation ... with the greatest vigilance and will take all measures that appear to be necessary for discouraging the spread of undesirable influences. [95]

The Loyalty League was so impressed by the confidential nature of Craigavon's response and by his message that it was more than happy to leave the matter in the government's hands.[96] However the fact that 'Ulster money' was still being spent on Irish rankled with loyalists and the issue eventually arose again. Meanwhile the position of Irish as an optional subject in public elementary schools had been clarified and slightly improved. It was now available from Standard III upwards and was not disadvantaged in comparison with other optional subjects. Trouble however loomed when loyalists realised in early 1933 that Irish could still be taught as an extra subject for fees.

In March 1933 William Grant MP, a thorn in the side of the pragmatists, discovered the existence of a new government regulation which reaffirmed the status of Irish as a fee-paying extra subject and raised the matter in parliament.[97] He began by asking Robb, the Parliamentary Secretary, to confirm the existence of this new regulation from which, he said rather pointedly, 'may be seen the attitude of the northern government ... towards the teaching of Irish in public elementary schools'. He also wanted to know if Latin and French had also been included amongst the extra subjects immediately prior to this; if these were now thought no longer worthy of study; and if Irish alone was considered of sufficient importance to warrant the payment of fees.

In reply Robb agreed that the new regulation did exist but explained that no fees had been paid for the teaching of Latin or French in 25 years. Grant's response was to attack the funding of Irish as an extra subject, and ask,

> ... is the hon. and learned Gentleman aware that the only people interested in this language are the people who are the avowed enemies of Northern Ireland - and does he not think the time has now arrived when this grant should be cut off? [98]

The government was now facing a problem. One of its influential loyalist supporters was accusing it of disloyalty. This could not be easily ignored.

A week later Grant returned to the attack, asking Robb how much per annum in special fees was paid for Irish instruction, the names of the schools involved and the amount paid to each school. He also wanted to know why there was a distinction in favour of Irish as against French, German and other useful languages and whether the Ministry would, in view of the fact that Irish had no commercial or business value in any part of the world, consider the advisability of discontinuing the payment of fees.[99]

The essence of Robb's response was that because Irish had occupied a peculiar and special position in the schools prior to the establishment of the Ministry, it had been decided, after very careful consideration, that it was desirable to continue the system of paying fees for the teaching of the language as an extra subject though on a more limited scale. He justified this by saying that the commercial value of a subject was not the only consideration in drawing up the most appropriate syllabus but that regard should also be given to the general educational and cultural interests involved.[100] In other words, the Ministry was, for the moment, upholding the new regulation in so far as it affected Irish.

In Stormont, five days later, the government's Irish-language policy was attacked again, this time by Tommy Henderson, an independent Unionist who had a large following of grassroots loyalists. He was an even greater threat to the government than Grant because his position outside the Party made him a potential rallying point for disaffected unionists who feared betrayal. He began by asking Robb what earthly good, use or purpose could be served in compelling children or teachers to learn Irish. When Robb denied that there was any compulsion, Henderson made an impassioned speech condemning government policy towards Irish. He accused the government of throwing money away by assisting children to learn Irish so that they could find employment in the Irish Free State, and continued,

> If I was to go up the Shankill Road and say I was going to learn Irish, I would be excommunicated. I would be chased. It would be looked on as a terrible crime if I were to learn Irish. Yet this very loyal Government are against the wishes of the people ...

When he discovered that £1,514 had been spent on Irish in the previous year he accused the government of not knowing where it stood on the Irish question and stressed the damage such a stance would cost at election time.

> This is a very serious matter, because 90% of the inhabitants of Northern Ireland are opposed to the Irish language. If I were to go to the hustings and say I supported the Government in spending £1,514 a year on the teaching of Irish to children of the elementary schools, what would happen? They would say I aided the Government in spending money on what was of no service. There are no signboards in Irish in Northern Ireland and why teach your children Irish. I believe it is compulsory in the Irish Free State, but we do not want it. [101]

The issue now became a matter of concern for the Cabinet. A month later Charlemont drew up for Craigavon a detailed memorandum on the teaching of Irish in public elementary schools. Apart from statistical information, it gave an interesting insight into the Ministry's willingness to support the teaching of Irish. The Ministry accepted that the subject had no commercial value and that it had little interest for Northern Ireland. However it recognised that Irish was the ancient language of Ireland and consequently had some claim to a special place in any system of education which included a knowledge of history and had regard to old local associations with archaeology, place-names and antiquities. The Ministry had therefore decided that although opportunities to teach Irish should be curtailed, the special position of the language should be recognised, particularly with reference to its status as an extra subject. Charlemont admitted that in the early days prohibition had not been considered for the reasons already given to the Loyalty League, but in this instance he offered another reason.

> The feeling of the Roman Catholic minority in regard to Irish was known to be acute, and if the cry could be raised that the language was persecuted by the Northern Government, the Ministry would be faced with an opposition which would cause a great amount of trouble and react prejudiciially on the progress and efficiency of the schools. For these reasons Lord Londonderry decided in 1923 that a middle course should be adopted and the teaching of Irish should be allowed to continue.

Turning to the current problem Charlemont proposed a simple solution - the abolition of fees for the teaching of Irish as an extra subject. He justified this on two counts, the relatively small numbers of pupils involved and the low level of interest generally in the study of Irish in Northern Ireland. Nevertheless he realised that an attack on the language might stimulate an interest in it. He recognised a similar danger when he suggested that fees might be abolished because too little time was being devoted to Irish to make the teaching effective. Advocates of the language might then urge the Ministry to extend the time available to Irish in order to make the teaching more efficient. He then pointed out that a decision to abolish the fees could not take effect until the 1934-5 Estimates were considered and ended by defending his Ministry's current strategy.

> There is no doubt that the fact that some recognition is given to Irish by the Ministry has greatly disarmed criticism on the part of anti-British elements in the population, while the actual results in spreading a knowledge of the language are insignificant. [102]

Charlemont then wrote a short letter to Craigavon which contained a few extra points. His first concern was that the Prime Minister should persuade Grant and his friends not to raise the question of grants for Irish again during the debate on the Education Estimates in return for an undertaking that they would be withdrawn the following year. It was not the grants that concerned him (in fact, he admitted that he did not care two pins about them); it was the conflict of interest between the government and Grant. According to him, one wanted to avoid the cry of injustice from the nationalists and the other wanted to avoid the promulgation of the Irish language. He seemed resigned to the fact that no choice existed but made the point that a negative policy could be counter-productive.

> Now if you want to make any sort of Irishman <u>do</u> something the surest way is to tell him that it's forbidden, and if the learning of the Irish language is a <u>bad</u> thing (I don't know that it is; it must be good for the brain to learn to remember that 'John Robb' is 'Eoin

Robbhch' [sic] and things like that) - if it's a <u>bad</u> thing, all I can say is that forbidding it under pressure will stimulate it to such an extent that the very dogs in Belfast - at any rate, the Falls Road dogs - will bark in Irish.

He suggested that if the grants were to be abolished, economic measures could be used as an excuse and perhaps something else could be withdrawn to take the edge off it. Finally he said that he had told Robb to give Grant the undertaking, if asked, and that he himself might see Grant about it the following Tuesday. Meanwhile Craigavon circulated Charlemont's memorandum amongst the Cabinet with a note to the effect that Robb, during his introductory remarks on the Education Estimates on the following Tuesday, would announce that the government on economic grounds would be unable to continue the payment of grants for the teaching of Irish as an extra subject beyond the school year ending in June 1934.[103]

On 25 April 1933, during the debate at the Committee stage of the Estimates, Robb made his announcement to cries of 'Hear! Hear!' from the Unionist Members. Payment of grants was to cease, not after June 1934, but after June 1933 - the very month the new regulation was issued. Government policy had been reversed. It was another tactical retreat for the pragmatists in the face of loyalist pressure.[104]

The Nationalist benches were not only silent, they were empty and had been since May 1932 when Nationalist Members, in frustration, had staged a walkout and maintained a boycott of parliamentary business which continued until October 1933.[105] Their presence would have made little difference. They already knew from bitter experience that the essential dynamic of the Unionist state gave them little scope for meaningful participation in its political affairs except as a threat to be exploited. Their ability to influence government decision-making positively was minimal and their role in parliament scarcely got beyond the documentation of nationalist grievances and fruitless arguments with government supporters. After 1933 the government's negative policy towards Irish featured more frequently in issues raised by Nationalist MPs. This, in turn, produced a predictably hostile or patronising unionist response.

On 12 March 1936 Robb, in answer to a parliamentary question, described Irish as a foreign language.[106] The Nationalist response was to raise the matter with the Prime Minister. Some days later T. J. Campbell, the Nationalist member for Belfast, Central, referring to political support in Britain for Welsh, asked the Prime Minister if he had been consulted before a recent regulation had categorised Irish as a foreign language and if he would consider rescinding it. Robb replied first, explaining that the last regulations made affecting the status of Irish were those of June 1933.[107]

The Prime Minister's opportunity to respond came later that day when Campbell raised the issue again. The MP attacked the Ministry of Education for its unfair treatment of Irish and its action in ranking Irish as a foreign language. It revealed, he said, a provincialism and obscurantism that was almost unthinkable and referred to the absolute pettiness of the Ministry in ending the £1,500 grant towards the teaching of Irish. He then challenged Robb to tell the Welsh soldiers currently stationed in Belfast that Welsh, too, was a foreign language in Wales and reminded the House that 90% of the placenames in Northern Ireland were Irish. Only philistines and withered pedagogues, he maintained, would try to degrade Irish. Finally, he declared defiantly that the Irish people need not despair at the attitude of the Ministry, that they would survive it and that in time they would also defeat the Parliamentary Secretary of the Ministry of Education.[108]

The Prime Minister's reply was patronising.

> I rather enjoyed the concluding remarks made by the hon. and learned Member when he stuck up, as I would always do, for our own country and I appreciated his historical reminiscences with regard to the Irish and the Irish language. I appreciated to the full the sentiment which he expressed so charmingly. But I would ask

him one question. What use is it to us here in this progressive, busy part of the Empire to teach our children the Irish language? What use would it be to them? Is it not leading them along a road which has no practical value? We have not stopped such teaching … We have stopped the grants simply because we do not see that these boys being taught Irish would be any better citizens … the Government have not any idea whatever of changing their minds in so far as giving a subsidy towards the teaching of Irish is concerned. I hope the hon. and learned Member is satisfied that on the whole the Government is carrying out its duties fairly and justly among all sections of the population. [109]

In March 1937, seven months before he replaced Charlemont as Minister of Education, Robb was asked if he had the good sense and the good taste to express regret for his statement that Irish was a foreign language in Northern Ireland. He replied without hesitation, 'No. I do not feel it nor shall I express it.' [110]

Following Robb's appointment, Mrs Dehra Parker, who as Dehra Chichester had expressed such animosity towards Irish in her reservations to the Lynn Report, became his Parliamentary Secretary. At this point it seemed unlikely that the existing regulations affecting Irish could generate any more controversy. The interplay between pragmatists and loyalists had brought unionist policy with regard to Irish in education to a state of delicate equilibrium. It was negative but not openly in contravention of norms acceptable to London. Nevertheless it was very much out of step with the positive policies of the British Board of Education towards Welsh which were gradually gathering momentum.

To pursue a more negative agenda towards Irish ran the risk of overtly breaking with accepted British standards in a sensitive area unrelated to security. This could upset relations with Britain and create unnecessary tensions in Northern Ireland when the United Kingdom was facing war with Germany. Paradoxically loyalist preoccupations with Catholic nationalist disloyalty might then be construed as another form of disloyalty by London if they were seen to take precedence over British interests at a time of national crisis. This message was slow to reach the unionist rank and file.

In the summer of 1942 the Unionist-controlled Strabane and Castlederg Regional Education Committee refused to accede to the request of 106 local students to establish an Irish class at Strabane Technical School, although the teaching of the subject was permissible according to the regulations. The incident developed into a major controversy which culminated in the dismissal of the principal of the Technical School who had recommended that the class be established.[111] Unionist reaction went beyond Strabane. It eventually reached the Grand Orange Lodge of Ireland in the form of the following resolution: 'That the Government of Northern Ireland be asked to remove from the Curriculum of the Ministry of Education the Irish language, and that no facilities be given in public, secondary or elementary schools for the teaching of such'.[112]

The new Prime Minister, J. M. Andrews, who was present at the Grand Lodge meeting when the resolution was discussed, promised Joseph Davison, the Grand Master, that he would look into the matter to see how far the wishes of the Grand Lodge could be followed.[113] On 17 December he sent a copy of the resolution to Robb with a note explaining his own view.

> I, personally, feel strongly that the teaching of Irish - the chief object of which is to foment antagonism to Great Britain and the second to gain a preference for those possessing this knowledge to obtain employment ... in Eire - should not be paid for by us.

He also wanted Robb to tell him what to say in reply.[114]

Ministry officials at once began gathering information to brief their Minister. Amongst their papers was an interesting circular from the Welsh Department of the British Board of Education which was quickly examined by eleven of the most senior officials in the Ministry including the Permanent Secretary. It was a glowing report on the efforts of the Board to encourage and support the teaching of Welsh in the schools of

Wales. It even included the text of an apology made to the Welsh people in the British House of Commons by the President of the Board on behalf of the government for its negative attitude towards Welsh during the previous century. [115]

On Christmas Eve 1942 the Permanent Secretary, R.S. Brownell, wrote a short briefing note to Robb. He recommended no change to the current position affecting Irish. The only alternative, he said, was to issue a regulation banning the teaching of Irish in schools. The result, he declared, would be disastrous.

> Such a regulation would merely have the effect of increasing the spread of the language in the Roman Catholic schools; without a doubt all the schools which at present teach it would continue to do so after school hours, they would be joined by others who at present don't bother about it; and a situation would develop which would be disastrous for Northern Ireland - all this at a time when the Board of Education is taking the most active steps to stimulate the learning of Welsh in the schools of Wales. [116]

A fortnight later, on 7 January 1943, Robb wrote to the Prime Minister. First, he gave him a summary of the current position with regard to the teaching of Irish in schools, emphasising that in all circumstances the regulations forbade any form of compulsion. Turning then to the Grand Lodge's resolution, he said that it was based not on educational but on political grounds and would involve the prohibition of Irish in schools. Dealing next with government educational policy which included Irish, he explained that it was based on the fundamental principle that when there was a demand for the teaching of any subject the demand should be met, so far as the course provider could do so reasonably within available resources. Moving on to the question of Irish he said that the demand for it was quite clear and that the language was also taught and examined in Queen's University, Trinity College, Dublin and the National University of Ireland. Then he mentioned that Gaelic was taught in Scottish universities, adding,

> ... and over and above that the Board of Education in England is at present busy with an effort to extend and develop the teaching of Welsh in Wales. For us now to forbid the teaching of Irish in our schools in face of the obvious demand for it would have a very awkward look.

Commenting next on the unionist view, shared by the Prime Minister, that Irish was demanded for political reasons, he said that there probably was an element of truth in it, but pointed out that past unionist agitation to have grants withdrawn from the subject had the opposite effect from the one intended, because it increased rather than decreased demand for the language in schools by drawing attention to it. Reiterating Brownell's warning that the complete prohibition of Irish would most likely boost the teaching of the language in schools, he revealed another danger,

> and [prohibition] would have this further disadvantage that whereas now, the books used are under our supervision, and are politically innocuous, then we should have no control whatever over books or courses of teaching.

He argued next that Catholic pupils needed to study Irish for certain careers including the priesthood and said that he could not see how the subject could be withdrawn when previous generations had had access to it. Finally, he declared forcefully,

> The position is this: the Manager of an elementary school or the Governors of a Secondary School may devote part of their pupils' time to learning Irish. If they do, in your opinion and mine the pupils might be much more usefully employed. But they do not think so, and the matter is one for them. Under our regulations we see that they do not make the subject obligatory and they must provide an alternative for any pupils not wishing to take it. But the choice is for them, and is part of that freedom of the individual for which we profess to be fighting this war. [117]

A week later the Prime Minister wrote to the Grand Master emphasising the dangers of prohibition,

> If we were to forbid the teaching of this subject, the effect would be that it would be taught somehow, somewhere, with no control over the books or the courses of instruction, and such a step, with the inevitable controversy which would arise, would probably have the effect of encouraging the teaching of Irish more generally and along lines much more detrimental to Ulster than at present.

Personally he would have been glad, he said, to have the teaching of Irish stopped altogether but informed Davison that it did not appear to be possible.[118]

Perhaps the irony of Unionist policy was lost on both but the lesson was learned at least in the case of Irish. Stalemate had been reached. From then on, Irish was grudgingly tolerated as a foreign language within the education system but, unlike other languages, was subject to periodic abuse from Unionist politicians.

Some unionists today seek to justify this negativity by holding nationalists responsible. They claim that at one stage the Irish language had a civic identity which made it accessible to them and blame Catholic nationalism alone for denying them access to it later by giving it a political identity which excluded them.[119] This is, perhaps, too simplistic. It is clear from Charlemont's remarks that, in the years immediately after partition, some influential unionists accepted that Irish, as the ancient language of Ireland, deserved a special place in the education system of the new northern state in spite of militant Catholic nationalism. Undoubtedly the movement away from this position had much to do with unionist perceptions of Catholic nationalists, but it owes more to the internal dynamics of unionism than unionists in general are prepared to admit.

Footnotes

1. *Memorandum*, Public Record Office of Northern Ireland (PRONI) CAB5/1.

2. Sir James Craig, *Appreciation of the situation in* Ulster, Admiralty, 1 September 1920, PRONI CAB 5/1; see also T. Jones (ed. K. Middlemas), *Whitehall Diary*, Vol III: *Ireland 1918-1925*, London:

Oxford University Press, 1971: 38.

3. See P. J. Corish, 'The Cromwellian regime, 1650-60', in T.W. Moody et al., eds, *A New History of Ireland*, Vol III: *Early Modern Ireland 1534-1691*, Oxford: Clarendon Press, 1976: 368; see also 5 below.

4. M. Farrell, *Arming the Protestants: the Formation of the Ulster Special Constabulary and the Royal Ulster Constabulary 1920-27*, Dingle: Brandon, 1983: 279-80.

5. For example see G. E. Aylmer, *Rebellion or Revolution? England 1640-1660*, Oxford: Oxford University Press, 1986: 30, 68; T. Bartlett, *The Fall and Rise of the Catholic Nation: the Catholic Question 1690-1830*, Dublin: Gill and Macmillan, 1992: 235; and F. Wright, *Two Lands on One Soil: Ulster Politics before Home Rule*, Dublin: Gill and Macmillan, 1996: 282-3, 298, 316-17, 404, 432.

6. *Northern Whig,* 13 July 1920.

7. E. Phoenix, *Northern Nationalism: Nationalist Politics, Partition and the Catholic Minority in Northern Ireland 1890-1940*, Belfast: Ulster Historical Foundation, 1994: 87-88.

8. M. Farrell, op. cit.: 36-50, 187-195.

9. P. Bew, P. Gibbon, H. Patterson, *The State in Northern Ireland 1921-72: Political Forces and Social Classes*, Manchester: Manchester University Press, 1979: 83.

10. E. Phoenix, op. cit.: 243.

11. M. Farrell, op. cit.: 280.

12. M. Ó Murchú, *The Irish Language*, Dublin: Department of Foreign Affairs/Bord na Gaeilge, 1985: 27-8.

13. See J. T. Leerssen, *Mere Irish and Fíor-Ghael: Studies in the Idea of Irish Nationality, its Development and Literary Expression prior to the Nineteenth Century*, Amsterdam: John Benjamins, 1986: 325-7, 332, 402-6, 417-40.

14. R. Blaney, *Presbyterians and the Irish Language,* Belfast: Ulster Historical Foundation, 1996: 13-16.

15. See J. T. Leerssen, op. cit.: 327-30; and R. Blaney, op. cit.: 20-27, 69-

70, 76-82.

16. G. Ó Tuathaigh, 'Maigh Nuad agus stair na Gaeilge', in E. Ó Siocháin, ed., *Maigh Nuad: Saothru na Gaeilge 1795-1995*, Maynooth: An Sagart, 1995: 13-14.

17. J. Hutchinson, *The Dynamics of Cultural Nationalism: the Gaelic Revival and the Creation of the Irish Nation State*, London: Allen & Unwin, 1987: 94, 141.

18. B. Ó Buachalla, *I mBéal Feirste Cois Cuain*, Dublin: Clóchomhar, 1968: 272.

19. See J. Loughlin, *Gladstone, Home Rule and the Ulster Question 1882-93*, Dublin: Gill and Macmillan, 1986: 20; J. Hutchinson, op. cit.: 121-2, 136-140.

20. G. Grote, *Torn Between Politics and Culture: The Gaelic League 1893-1993*, Münster/New York: Waxmann, 1994: 24.

21. B. Ó Cuív, *Irish Dialects and Irish-Speaking Districts*, Dublin: Dublin Institute for Advanced Studies, 1951: 27.

22. *The Case for Ulster Irish on Ulster Radio and Television: Report by a Study Group*, Belfast: Gaelic League, 1978: 18.

23. *Census of Ireland, 1911: Province of Ulster*, Dublin, 1912: 59.

24. D. Greene, 'The Irish language movement' in M. Hurley, ed., *Irish Anglicanism 1869-1969*, Dublin: Allen Figgis, 1970: 114-116.

25. 'Organised Orange ruffianism: cowardly attack on Catholics at Ballyward, Co. Down', *Irish Weekly*, 19 August 1905.

26. 'Chief Secretary and the Gaelic League', *Irish Weekly*, 27 May 1905.

27. T. W. Moody and J.C. Beckett, *Queen's Belfast: the History of a University*, London: QUB/Faber & Faber, 1959: 413.

28. S. Mac Mathúna and R. Mac Gabhann, *Conradh na Gaeilge agus an tOideachas Aosach*, Indreabhán: Cló Chois Fharraige, 1981: 119.

29. D. Ó Suilleabháin, *Cath na Gaeilge sa Chóras Oideachais 1893-1911*, Dublin: Conradh na Gaeilge, 1988: passim.

30. M. Ní Mhuiríosa, *Réamhchonraitheoirí*, Dublin: Clódhanna Teoranta, 1968: 7-10.

31. See *Instruction in Irish in Northern Ireland National Schools*, 1921, PRONI ED13/1/878.

32. *ibid.*, PRONI ED13/1/878.

33. See S. Ó Buachalla, 'An Ghaeilge sa chóras oideachais', *Comhar*, 31(5), Bealtaine 1972: 10; see also *An Coimisiún um Athbheochan na Gaeilge: an Tuarascáil Dheiridh*, Dublin: Government Publications' Office, 1963: 19.

34. PRONI ED13/1/1598; Robb mentions 242 schools, see 90 below.

35. C. Ó Cearúil, *Aspail ar son na Gaeilge: Timirí na Gaeilge 1899-1923*, Dublin: Conradh na Gaeilge, 1995: 98.

36. See S. Farren, *The Politics of Irish Education 1920-65*, Belfast: QUB Institute of Irish Studies, 1996: 36-7.

37. See M. Harris, *The Catholic Church and the Foundation of the Northern Irish State*, Cork: Cork University Press, 1993: 92-96.

38. M. Farrell, *Northern Ireland: the Orange State*, London: Pluto Press, 1980: 93-5.

39. M. Harris, op.cit.: 145-9.

40. E. Phoenix, op. cit.: 380, 397-399.

41. See PRONI HA 5/1637; Mawhinney, a Presbyterian republican internee, was a science teacher at the Municipal Technical School, Derry. When he asked for books to study engineering subjects and Irish, an official wrote in his file (14 March 1923), 'I should be more inclined, if I were discriminating to preclude him from access to the books in "Irish" '. However, permission was granted.

42. *Parliament of Northern Ireland: Commons Debates* (PNICD) Vol. I, cols 520-1.

43. Reported in the *Irish News*, 4 February 1922.

44. *Cause for Teachers' Action*, PRONI T2886.

45. E. Phoenix, op. cit.: 211.

46. Collins to Londonderry, 10 April 1922, PRONI ED/32/B/1/2/52.

47. PNICD Vol II, col. 525.

48. Modifications of School Programmes, Wyse to Senior Chief

Inspector, 10 August 1922, PRONI ED13/1/878.

49. Colleges for the Teaching of Irish, Wyse to Secretary, 10 August 1922, PRONI ED13/1/878.

50. See PRONI ED32/B/1/2/123; Phoenix, op. cit.: 249.

51. Macaulay and Hendley to McQuibban, 11 September 1922, PRONI ED32/B/1/2/123.

52. Memorandum (n.d.), PRONI ED32/B/1/2/123.

53. *ibid.*, PRONI ED32/B/1/2/123.

54. See 52 above.

55. Garrett and Welply to Wyse, 8 September 1922, PRONI ED13/1/878.

56. See 51 above.

57. McQuibban to Lord Londonderry, 15 September 1922, PRONI ED 32/B/1/2/123.

58. A note from Wyse to McQuibban dated 11 November 1922, written on the report; see 55 above.

59. See E. Phoenix, op. cit.: 258.

60. See J. L. Fitts, *The Rebel Teachers: A Study in Contentious History*, unpublished monograph, San Luis Obispo: California Polytechnic State University (n. d.): 39-41; see also P. Mac Con Midhe, 'Stair na Gaeilge i scoileanna na Sé gContae', *An tUltach*, 48(5), Bealtaine 1971: 5.

61. McQuibban to Londonderry, 11 November 1922, PRONI ED13/1/878.

62. 'Accepting the inevitable', *Belfast Newsletter*, 1 December 1922.

63. S. Farren, 'Teacher education: the collapse of its all-Ireland dimension in 1922', *Irish Educational Studies*, 7(2), 1988: 24, 29.

64. PNICD Vol. III, cols 663-4.

65. PNICD Vol. III, cols 1090-93.

66. *Final Report of the Departmental Committee on the Educational Services in Northern Ireland*, Belfast: HMSO, 1923: 55.

67. *ibid.*: 49-50.

68. *ibid.*: 83.

69. *ibid., loc. cit.*

70. *Programme of Instruction for Public Elementary Schools for the School Year 1924-25*, Belfast: HMSO, 1924: 9.

71. See INTO submission dated 16 May 1924, PRONI ED13/1/812.

72. See statistics for 1924-25 in PRONI ED13/1/516 and for 1927-28 in PRONI ED13/1/1598.

73. *Report of the Ministry of Education for the Year 1924-25*: 65.

74. See handwritten note on McQuibban to Yates, 12 August 1925, PRONI ED13/1/516.

75. *Parliament of Northern Ireland: Senate Debates*, Vol. 7, col. 123.

76. S. R. & O. (NI) 1926, No. 45.

77. *Report of the Ministry of Education for the Year 1927-28*: 20.

78. A. Ó Muimhneacháin, *Dóchas agus Duainéis: Scéal Chonradh na Gaeilge 1922-1932*, Cork: Mercier, 1975: 146-153.

79. *Notes of an Interview at the Ministry of Education on Tuesday 1st February, 1927, with a Deputation in Connection with the Facilities given for Instruction in Irish in Public Elementary Schools*, PRONI ED13/1/516.

80. J.F. Charles, 'Gaelic in Ulster: the thin end of the wedge', *Northern Whig*, 20 June 1927.

81. Wilson to Robb, 21 June 1922, PRONI ED32/B/1/2/60.

82. Charlemont to Hungerford, 28 June 1927, PRONI ED32/B/1/2/60.

83. Hungerford to Charlemont, 1 July 1927, PRONI ED32/B/1/2/60; see also 'The teaching of Irish: to the editor of the Northern Whig', *Northern Whig*, 2 July 1927.

84. *Notes of an Interview at the Ministry of Education on Friday, 16th December, 1927 with a Deputation Representing the Ulster Gaelic League*, PRONI ED13/1/516.

85. Wyse to Yates, 4 January 1928, PRONI ED13/1/516.
86. In the preamble to its aims and objectives the League declared its fundamental principle to be: 'To form a Society where membership is confined solely to men and women of British race and blood, which will work primarily for the benefit of that race, its Country and its Empire and which recognises, to obtain this end, alien races must be eliminated from all our Councils and National Institutions', PRONI CAB9D/44/1.
87. E.J. Wolfenden-Clarke to Craigavon, 9 June 1928, PRONI ED32/B/1/2/60.
88. Blackmore to Wyse, 11 June 1928, PRONI CAB 9D/44/1.
89. Robb mentioned the letter in Robb to Grant, 13 June 1928, PRONI ED32/B/1/2/60.
90. *ibid.*, PRONI ED32/B/1/2/60.
91. *Memorandum regarding the teaching of Irish in Public Elementary Schools and letter addressed to the Prime Minister by the Loyalty League dated 9 June, 1928*, PRONI CAB9D/44/1.
92. Wyse to Blackmore, 20 June 1928, PRONI ED32/B/1/2/60.
93. Blackmore to E. J. Clarke, 26 June 1928, PRONI CAB9D/44/1.
94. Clarke to Craigavon, 10 July 1928, PRONI CAB9D/44/1.
95. Taylor to Clarke, 20 August 1928, PRONI CAB 9D/44/1.
96. Clarke to Craigavon, 4 September 1928, PRONI CAB 9D/44/1.
97. S. R. & O. (NI) 1932, No. 113.
98. PNICD Vol.XV, col. 772.
99. PNICD Vol.XV, col. 918.
100. PNICD Vol.XV, cols 918-19.
101. PNICD Vol.XV, cols 960-1.
102. *Memorandum by the Minister of Education on the Teaching of Irish in Public Elementary Schools*, 21 April 1933, PRONI CAB 9D/44/1.
103. Charlemont to Craigavon, 22 April 1933, PRONI CAB 9D/44/1.
104. PNICD Vol.XV, cols 1076-8.

105. M. Farrell, op. cit., 1980: 118, 142.
106. PNICD Vol.XVIII, col. 567.
107. PNICD Vol.XVIII, cols 631-2.
108. PNICD Vol.XVIII, col. 642.
109. PNICD Vol.XVIII cols 645-6.
110. PNICD Vol.XIX, col. 677.
111. See PNICD Vol.XXV, col. 2706, 1711-14.
112. Davison to Andrews, 11 December 1942, PRONI CAB9D/44/1.
113. Andrews to Davison, 17 December 1942, PRONI CAB9D/44/1.
114. Andrews to Robb, 17 December 1942, PRONI CAB9D/44/1.
115. *The Teaching of Welsh, Wales: Circular 182*, 9 October 1942, PRONI CAB9D/44/1.
116. Brownell to Robb, 24 December 1942, PRONI ED 13/1/101.
117. Robb to Andrews, 7 January 1943, PRONI CAB 9D/44/1.
118. Andrews to Davison, 13 January 1943, PRONI CAB9D/44/1.
119. See, for example, S. King, 'The Irish language movement is allied to separatism', *Irish News*, 25 August 1997.

Acknowledgement

The author is grateful to the Deputy Keeper of the Records, the Public Record Office of Northern Ireland, for permission to quote from PRONI sources.

Nationalists and the Irish language in Northern Ireland: Competing Perspectives
CAMILLE O'REILLY

The Irish language has been an important issue in the history of Ireland for centuries. Today, although Irish people are Irish whether or not they can speak Gaelic, the language nevertheless occupies a special symbolic position in the definition of a distinctive Irish identity. Irish has had a significant formal status in the southern state since its inception. Irish has become an increasingly important aspect of the national identity of many nationalists in Northern Ireland as well, where the current resurgence of interest is probably the most vibrant and widespread this century. In spite of the broad support that the Irish language enjoys among nationalists in Northern Ireland, however, the symbolic and practical meanings of both the language and the revival are strongly contested. In this essay, I will explore a number of different perspectives on the Irish language currently held by nationalists in the north.

Attitudes to the Irish language cannot be separated from the immediate social and political context of Northern Ireland. Even though the remaining population of native Irish speakers in the six counties of Ulster which became Northern Ireland had largely disappeared by the time of partition, the Irish language movement survived and occasionally thrived. In a society which is fundamentally divided on political grounds, to learn or speak Irish is perceived as an act with political implications. Those who chose to do so inevitably have to define their own sense of how the language relates to their political identity. Different perspectives on the Irish language also have deep historic roots within Northern Ireland and in the island as a whole. Current attitudes towards the language owe much to the different ways in which that history is interpreted. Supporters of the language point out that the historic role of Irish in Belfast and the north has often been ignored in 'official' versions of history. They believe that it is important to assert that Irish has always been a part of what is now Northern Ireland, and place great emphasis on the many revival activities which have been based in Belfast since the eighteenth century. The city has often been an important centre of the Irish language movement for the island as a whole.

Competing interpretations of history and society both reflect and affect the distribution and exercise of power within society. The attitudes and relationship of Irish speakers to power structures are often reflected in the very language they use when talking about Irish. One powerful tool for interpreting people's beliefs about Irish, and the implications of those beliefs, is to examine their discourses, or ways of talking about the language.

A discourse can be identified by certain words or phrases which characterize that particular way of talking, or by certain patterns of speech. For example, the discourse of football commentary includes 'hat trick,' 'goal' and 'offside,' while the discourse of cookery includes 'teaspoonful' and 'bring to the boil.' None of us would have much trouble distinguishing between a sermon, a news report and a comedy routine after listening for just a few seconds or reading just a few lines. This is due in part to the different discourses used in each of these ways of talking.

Discourse refers to much more than just patterns of speech, however. It is a linguistic vehicle for thought, emotions and ideologies. Successfully putting across your ideas or beliefs through discourse, and having those ideas accepted, is a form of power. Some theorists (notably Foucault 1972, 1982) see dominant discourses – frameworks of ideas which are unthinkingly accepted by those who use them – as means of perpetuating and reproducing particular ideologies and power relationships. My own conception of the way discourses are used is less rigid and 'top down,' and tends towards a more dynamic model. The ideology we use to express our experience of social reality is formed within the framework of existing discourses and is constrained by them, but it is also modified by the process of discourse. Discourses do not simply reflect the way people feel or what they believe – they are the place where these feelings and beliefs are actually formed and reformed, supported and challenged. In the process of speaking or writing, we all participate actively in the creation, reproduction and change of ideas and beliefs.

If the function of a dominant discourse is to legitimize a particular set of power relations, it can be challenged by two separate processes. By engaging creatively with the dominant discourse within its own terms of reference, the discourse itself, and the power relationships it embodies, can be changed. On the other hand, a dominant discourse can be delegitimized or challenged through the failure to engage with it, or through the conscious use of alternative discourses.

Both of these processes are at work within the discourses of the Irish language movement in Northern Ireland. Some directly challenge the legitimacy of the discourses which are directly linked with institutions of power. Others, while challenging those same institutions, are used within acceptably defined parameters of debate – for example the issue of 'parity of esteem'[1] or comparisons between the status of Irish and other minority languages in the United Kingdom. Certain aspects of some Irish language discourses have already been incorporated into the dominant discourses, particularly those linked to the discourses of community relations and cultural diversity. There is an ongoing process of negotiation taking place between the different discourses within the Irish language movement itself, and between the language movement and the dominant discourses. Recent attempts to construct a peace process may result in even more of these discourses being adopted by the institutions of power in Northern Irish society.

Three discourses

Talk by nationalists about the Irish language in Northern Ireland can be divided into three separate discourses. While this breakdown is not exhaustive of all possibilities, it is representative of the bulk of nationalist opinion on the language. I have labelled these three ways of talking about the Irish language decolonizing discourse, cultural discourse, and rights discourse. Although individuals often mix discourses to suit their own purposes, for the sake of clarity I will focus on talk which draws primarily from just one discourse, looking at each of the three discourses in turn.

Decolonizing discourse is often associated with Sinn Féin, although they by no means have a monopoly on the point of view associated with this discourse. Irish gained a very high profile during the hunger strike in 1981, partly because the first man to die, Bobby Sands, was an Irish speaker, and partly due to the increasingly widespread use of the Irish language to communicate amongst republican prisoners in Long Kesh. Sinn Féin's involvement with the Irish language throughout the 1980s contributed a great deal to the current shape of decolonizing discourse, which is perhaps best typified by much of the rhetoric of Sinn Féin and a number of its prominent members.

The story does not begin there, however. At least since the major split in the Gaelic League which culminated in the resignation of Douglas Hyde from his position as president in 1915, there has been an ideological division between those who made a strong association between the Irish language and the political independence of Ireland, and those who sought to keep politics outside of efforts to revive the language. Michael Collins is one republican leader from the time of the Easter Rising who strongly associated the language with independence for Ireland. His words articulate the belief at the foundation of much of decolonizing discourse:

> We only succeeded after we had begun to get back our Irish ways;

after we had made a serious effort to speak our own language; after we had striven again to govern ourselves. We can only keep out the enemy and all other enemies by completing that task ... The biggest task will be the restoration of the Irish language (quoted in Ó Fiaich 1969: 111).

The following quote is an example of what I would now call decolonizing discourse. It demonstrates the historical roots of this discourse and the manner in which it is expressed quite clearly. The quote is taken from an article written under the *nom de plume* Fergus MacLede and published under the title 'The Gaelic League and Politics' in the September 1913 issue of the journal *Irish Freedom:*

> The English have long bent their energies to the conquest of Ireland ... Their dangerous assault has been on the language, the mould of our distinctive native civilisation ... The work of the Gaelic League is to prevent the assimilation of the Irish nation by the English nation ...
>
> The Gaelic League does not stand to take sides in the political differences that separate Irishmen into different parties, and therefore it is claimed to be non–political. This claim can only be upheld by twisting the plain meaning of the words ... It has confused the one straight issue for them, and that straight issue is whether the Irish nation or the English nation is to predominate in Ireland ... The Irish language is a political weapon of the first importance against English encroachment ... (quoted in Ó Huallacháin 1994: 66–67).

The discourse in this quote bears some striking resemblances to decolonizing discourse as it is used today. It is important to realize, however, that decolonizing discourse in its present form is not simply a repetition of the words of the past, such as those quoted above. The words are similar, but used in the current social and political context of Northern Ireland they take on new meanings and new implications. There is an illusion of historical continuity promoted by the obvious surface similarities in discourse, past and present, which is important in establishing both credibility and a sense of community and history, at least among those who subscribe to the ideologies expressed through and created by this discourse.

In the first half of the 1980s, decolonizing discourse was associated with quite an extreme ideology. Irish was literally seen as a weapon in the arsenal available to fight the British. A well known statement demonstrates this position. A prominent member of Sinn Féin, who is also an Irish language activist, has been quoted as saying 'Every word of Irish spoken is like another bullet being fired in the struggle for Irish freedom.' In the course of its development, decolonizing discourse seems to have been somewhat moderated. It would be somewhat unusual, for example, to hear someone make such a statement today. Although the most extreme versions of this discourse may be in retreat, the belief that the Irish language has an important political role and significance is still widespread, and this discourse is still drawn upon by some people in particular circumstances.

The fundamental difference in each of the three discourses lies in the way in which the relationship between the Irish language and politics is conceptualized. In decolonizing discourse, Irish is made an integral part of party politics in general and republicanism in particular, identified as part of the process of decolonization. There is a strong naturalization of the connection with nationalism, and a strong connection with the republican struggle. The Irish language tends to be seen as inherently political.

Certain key words, concepts and arguments indicate the use of decolonizing discourse: 'resistance' or 'cultural resistance,' 'oppression,' 'reconquest,' Irish as a 'weapon,' cultural 'struggle,' particularly as part of a wider anti–colonial struggle, and 'republican,' or a strong association made with republican ideals or beliefs. Discourses of anti–imperialism, de–colonization, or political struggle are frequently used in association with the Irish language. Connections are often explicitly made between a person's nationalist political deveiopment and his or her interest in the language. Speaking and learning Irish are seen as political acts. Speaking Irish is also seen as a particularly powerful expression of national, and not simply ethnic, identity.

The following examples illustrate these points. One man in his twenties told me:

> I first got interested in Irish through politics. Everything I'm interested in stems from the politics I have. My introduction to anything cultural would be through politics. ... You can define struggle in different ways, and the importance of the Irish language came to the fore through Bobby Sands and the *Gaeltachts* in the jail. ... The people who came out of the jails were people you could relate to ... Maybe your best friend went to jail and came out as an Irish speaker and that would influence you, you know what I mean?

When asked why she became involved with the Irish language, a young woman put it this way: 'I felt that with the struggle going on for nationalists to free themselves, I felt that it was a good chance for me to play my part in the culture, more so than in the military.' [2]

A Sinn Féin leaflet from the mid–1980s describes the situation regarding the language this way:

> Sinn Féin proclaimed loudly that the language question was political or that it was because of a political decision that Irish was taken from us in the first place.
>
> People must recognise that the anti–Irish campaign is interwoven with the British presence in Ireland. Irish people need to recognise that Irish will not magically reappear when the Brits go. The language suffered after the English came and it will recover before they leave. We also have to accept that having the language back will help bring an end to the foreign rule in Ireland. As the Irish influence rises, the foreign influence decreases.

On the other side of the ideological fence from decolonizing discourse is cultural discourse. The clearest and most dominant feature of cultural discourse is the assertion that the Irish language and politics should be kept separate. The corollary is that the importance of the language lies in its beauty and cultural worth, not its political capital. What exactly is meant by 'politics', however, is not generally made explicit. Often the word 'political' is used as a synonym for 'republican.' When a person says the language should be kept apolitical, they are often making a veiled comment on the perceived relationship of the Irish language to republicanism, usually casting it in an unfavourable light.

Another common implicit meaning of 'politics' is party politics, or more specifically, sectarian politics. In this case, the belief is that the language should not be used to further the ends of any one political party, or that Irish should be kept as far removed from sectarian politics as possible. In practice, though, this still usually refers to republican politics, because Sinn Féin tends to take a high profile position on Irish language issues. Political acts in support of the Irish language, for example lobbying the government in support of Irish medium education or campaigning for greater funding for the language, are not necessarily condemned and may even be condoned. Approval or disapproval of this type of political activity largely depends on the context and on who is doing the campaigning. Sinn Féin involvement might bring condemnation from some circles.

Like decolonizing discourse, cultural discourse has a relatively long history. Probably the best known advocate of this view of the Irish language was Douglas Hyde, president of the Gaelic League from its inception in 1893 until his resignation in 1915. According to Hutchinson (1987), Hyde was a cultural nationalist embroiled in a classic confrontation with political nationalists. While cultural nationalists believe that '... only by returning to their unique history and culture could Irish men and women realize their human potential and contribute to the wider European civilization,' political nationalists believe that '... only through the exercise of self–determination as citizens of an independent state could individuals find dignity' (Hutchinson 1987: 2). Hutchinson argues that the two forms of nationalism articulate different conceptions of the nation and have diverging political strategies, as Hyde found to his cost.

Hyde believed that for Irish to survive, it was essential to include people from all political persuasions in the revival movement. He tried to bring together all shades of nationalist and unionist opinion behind the common cause of the Irish language. However much the political pressure in favour of Home Rule increased, and in spite of the clear political implications of the activities of the Gaelic League during this politically charged period, Hyde continued to insist that his work and the work of the League were purely cultural (Dunleavy & Dunleavy 1991: 11). The pressure to make the Gaelic League overtly political increased during the period from 1910 to 1915. When Hyde felt that he could no longer keep the Gaelic League separate from the political maelstrom, he resigned from his position as president.

The powerful association between Irish nationalism and the Irish language remains to this day, and it has once again become a serious issue of debate. Interestingly, Hyde is used by people of many different political views to justify their own stance. Hyde has been used by nationalists and unionists alike to suggest that the language revival movement has been hijacked by republicans. He has been used by advocates of cultural discourse to prove that the Irish language is there for all the people of this island regardless of their political or religious persuasion, and used by some unionists to prove that Irish is indeed a republican language.

Cultural discourse today comes in two guises. In one guise it tends to be less political, drawing heavily from romantic and sometimes cultural nationalist ideals. An example of this version is the way a Belfast teacher explains his interest in learning Irish: 'I'd always promised myself to learn Irish and speak it, not through any sort of identity crisis, but because in it I find a certain inherent beauty and a different perspective for looking at the world.'

In its second guise cultural discourse has a clear political perspective of its own. The interplay between culture and identity is a key focus point. In some instances it is used as a political tool against decolonizing discourse, but its agenda is much broader than this. The focus on 'culture' is part of an attempt to create space for the growth and development of identities beyond the narrow boundaries which tend to confine definitions of 'nationalist' or 'unionist' culture. In this more political guise, cultural discourse often appears alongside the discourses of 'heritage' and 'tradition.' The Irish language has figured prominently in much of the discourse of Irish heritage, both in everyday speech and in 'official' quarters. Cultural discourse has been partly institutionalized under the auspices of 'heritage' through the Cultural Traditions Group (CTG), formally established in 1989 as a sub–committee of the government funded charity the Community Relations Council (CRC). The CRC is funded by the Central Community Relations Unit (CCRU), a section of the Department of Finance and Personnel. In this rather roundabout way, cultural discourse has been increasingly incorporated into the state discourses. It is increasingly necessary to use this type of discourse in order to obtain the support of major funding organizations, as well as local and national government.

The Irish language has been an important part of the CTG's work from the beginning, so much so that an Irish word has been incorporated into its official logo and a parallel organization, the ULTACH Trust, was set up to deal specifically with the language. The CTG produced a booklet entitled *Giving Voices* to review its development and accomplishments over the period 1990–94 in which it states: 'From the outset the new committee realised that it had to pass what was called the "green litmus test" – finding a credible policy on the Irish language' (CTG 1994: 6). Dr James Hawthorne, Chairman of the Community Relations Council, is quoted as saying:

> We strongly valued it [Irish] as a source of enrichment central to our cultural heritage. Indeed I believed that an effort must be made – by all sides – to release it from misunderstanding and

prejudice, not use it as mere graffiti to exclude, confuse or taunt others (CTG 1994: 6).

The place of the Irish language within the organization is revealed by Dr Maurice Hayes, chairman of the CTG from 1990–93:

> ... the main object [of the Cultural Traditions Group] is to promote discussion and debate about the validity of the various cultural traditions in Northern Ireland in a constructive and non–confrontational atmosphere. One shorthand was to help Protestants to contemplate the Irish language without necessarily feeling offended by it, or for Catholics to look on Orange processions without feeling intimidated. Of course this rather begs the question that some Orange processions are indeed intended to assert a claim to territory, or to superiority, and sometimes to intimidate, and *some manifestations of the Irish language are precisely employed in order to cause as much offence as possible to Unionists* (CTG 1994: 9; ULTACH Trust 1991; italics added).

In Hayes's view, the Irish language can be viewed as a kind of 'shorthand' for Catholic or nationalist culture, and presented to unionists as a non–threatening manifestation of that culture. This is not entirely consistent with the view expressed by Hawthorne above, where Irish is portrayed as belonging collectively to 'our' culture, presumably referring to a culture shared by both Catholics and Protestants. The problem is indicative of two conflicting versions of cultural traditions discourse. Hayes is drawing on the 'two traditions' version, while Hawthorne is using 'common heritage' discourse (cf. McCoy n.d.). This ambiguity in cultural traditions discourse[3] gives it a certain flexibility which not only helps to widen its appeal, but makes it more resistant to attack. Either version of cultural traditions discourse – or both – can be drawn upon depending on the context.

In the final sentence of the above quote, Hayes implicitly accuses at least some people of using the Irish language in an unacceptably political manner. The CTG makes a clear effort to place the Irish language firmly in the realm of culture and to 'release it from misunderstanding and prejudice, not use it as mere graffiti to exclude, confuse or taunt others' – in other words, they attempt to present the language in an inclusivist way in order to depoliticize it.

The idea of establishing an independent trust to promote the wider use of Irish came out of the 'Varieties of Irishness' conference organized by the CTG in 1989 (the proceedings of which were published – see Crozier 1989). The conference concluded that '...the language had unfortunately become associated with Republicanism in the eyes of many Protestants, which was a distortion of its real cultural significance' (CTG 1994:24). The following year, the issue of the Irish language was again discussed at the 'Varieties of Britishness' conference (see Crozier 1990). A seminar on law and administration concluded that 'statutory or financial impediments to the use of Irish should be removed to enable those who wished to use it to do so more freely,' while a seminar on educational issues said that 'Irish had suffered from being seen in a politicised context which alienated those who wanted to retain their Britishness' (CTG 1994: 24–25). According to the booklet *Giving Voices*, the CTG was 'quickly persuaded of *the need to confer a new legitimacy on its use and the study of its origins and dialects*, including its relationship to the Ulster–Scots tradition' (CTG 1994: 25, italics added). Here, 'to confer a new legitimacy' can be read as a euphemism for depoliticizing the language, or broadening its appeal.

Iontaobhas ULTACH/ ULTACH Trust was formed in 1989, opening an office in Belfast city centre in 1990. In April 1991, the British government agreed to contribute £250,000 to the Trust's capital fund, ensuring long–term viability and allowing the Trust to generate an independent income. Its remit is 'to promote the Irish language throughout the entire community of Northern Ireland.' One priority of the ULTACH Trust is '...to make [Irish] classes available in areas in which people from the Protestant community will not feel threatened and to help create an environment in which they can comfortably learn and use the language' (CTG 1994: 25). In practice this has sometimes been difficult to achieve. There is a great demand for funding and support for Irish language activities from people in the Catholic community who are already involved with the language, while on the Protestant side efforts are still being made to generate interest in Irish. This means that the Trust still funds a greater proportion of projects from the Catholic community, at the same time as it is working hard to implement its cross–community ideal.

Through the establishment of the Cultural Traditions Group and the ULTACH Trust, particular interpretations of the meaning and importance of the Irish language have become incorporated into discourses which are favoured by the state. This has profoundly affected the development of efforts to revive the Irish language in a number of ways. For the first time an organization has been funded by the British government with a remit exclusively devoted to the Irish language. The significance of Irish has been officially recognized, although in a particular way which attempts to dissociate the language from an exclusive nationalist identity. Perhaps even more importantly, one discourse of the Irish language has been given the official 'stamp of approval' and is now being used as the blueprint for further developments in relation to Irish. Effectively this means that other discourses are placed outside of circles of power, in opposition to cultural discourse which gains legitimacy by this association. Because cultural discourse is now associated with some of the primary sources of funding for the Irish language, it is becoming increasingly necessary to use this discourse in order to obtain financial support. Considering, however, that the symbolic meaning and importance of the language is so deeply contested, it is not surprising that there is still a great deal of debate on the issue. The image and meaning attributed to the Irish language by institutions associated with the government is considered more or less acceptable by the Irish language community depending on who you speak to.

As with decolonizing discourse, there are certain key words, concepts and arguments which indicate the use of cultural discourse: 'apolitical,' 'depoliticize,' 'inclusive,' 'tolerance,' 'understanding,' 'access,' 'multiculturalism,' 'pluralism,' 'beautiful language,' 'heritage' or 'common heritage' and 'cultural traditions' (as distinct from traditions). Cultural discourse is often used in conjunction with the discourse of community relations. Accusations that the language is being politicized, or attacks on specific individuals or groups for politicizing Irish, figure prominently. A connection is frequently made between a person's interest in Irish and its history, songs and literature. Speaking Irish is generally seen as a cultural activity, and it tends to be seen as an expression of ethnic or cultural identity (in contrast to the more dangerous and divisive political or nationalist expressions of identity).

If decolonizing and cultural discourses can be seen as constituting two sides of a debate about the relationship between politics and the Irish language, then rights discourse can be seen as a means to sidestep this debate and to open up new ideological avenues. In rights discourse, there are two key, inter–connected elements which make it less straightforward than the other two discourses. The first element centres around efforts to break out of the confines of the political/apolitical dichotomy established by the first two discourses. In these discourses the terms of debate are more or less agreed – Should politics be kept separate from the Irish language, or is the language an integral part of political struggle? In the third discourse, issues which lead into political/apolitical deadlock are sidestepped through a variety of different strategies, for example 'you can't hijack a language...' or arguments favouring the 'multipoliticization' of Irish, as well as other techniques of avoidance.

The second element centres around efforts to broaden and reframe the debate over politics and the Irish language. In recent years this has been achieved primarily through the issue of rights for Irish speakers. Discourses of civil rights, human rights and minority rights have been adapted as a means of campaigning for the language and developing an ideology which attempts to break out of the confines of the political/apolitical dichotomy.

For example, there is a common accusation made in some Irish language circles that Sinn Féin have 'hijacked' the language for their own political ends without genuine regard for the effect it might have on the language. A person who favours cultural discourse might agree with this statement, while someone who favours decolonizing discourse is likely to disagree. The most likely response of someone who favours rights discourse is to refute the idea that a language can be hijacked in the first place.

In a sense, people who say 'you can't hijack a language' are deliberately misunderstanding the accusation as a means of moving outside the restrictive framework of the debate. To address the accusation directly would mean becoming trapped in the political/apolitical dichotomy, so an alternative strategy of avoidance is used. The language as a symbol can, of course, be 'hijacked' in the sense that any symbol can be invested with new meanings. People who use this strategy, however, choose in this context to view Irish strictly as a language which anyone can learn or speak. In so doing, they implicitly deny its symbolic significance, at least in this context.

Inevitably, perhaps, the first two discourses have developed in close relationship with each other. Fairclough points out that 'discourse types tend to turn particular ways of drawing upon conventions and texts into routines, and to naturalize them' (1992: 85). The ideologies of cultural and decolonizing discourses tend to manifest themselves as two opposing sides of a debate, and they carry with them an enormous amount of other ideological baggage. If a person draws too heavily or obviously from either discourse, it tends to imply that he or she agrees with the associated ideologies.

It seems that in recent years people have begun to see the

existing conventions of the political/apolitical debate as overly restrictive and not representative of the way they were feeling about the Irish language and the political situation. It has become clear, for example, that many people see the Irish language as significant to their own political beliefs and to the political situation in Northern Ireland as a whole, without seeing the language in direct association with republicanism. This is problematic if the accepted conventions of discourse fix the language in either an apolitical position, or as an important element of cultural resistance to British rule as defined by republicanism. Challenges to this dichotomy have made it easier to express a view associating Irish with politics in the wider sense, without automatically being associated with republicanism. Instead of being depoliticized, the ideological associations made with the Irish language are being expanded and 'multipoliticized.'

With its emphasis on pragmatics and on the survival of the language, rights discourse is the most important medium of 'multipoliticization.' Indeed, this discourse does tend to be used in a very political way. In terms of party politics, users of rights discourse often justify making Irish part of a party political agenda – in fact, they tend to encourage all parties to do so as a means of promoting Irish, multipoliticizing it, and/or weakening the connection made between Irish and Sinn Féin. In terms of the relationship between politics in general and the language, there is some naturalization of the connection to nationalism, but also attempts to break this connection and widen the appeal of Irish. It is neither pro– nor anti–republican, this debate being sidestepped and reframed as described above. Speaking Irish is seen as a right, a form of freedom of expression. In keeping with the notion that associations with the language ought to be broadened, individuals may see speaking Irish as an expression of national, ethnic, or cultural identity, or a combination of these.

Talk of civil rights for Irish speakers is commonly associated with rights discourse, especially with reference to the funding of Irish schools and the right to use Irish when in contact with the state (for example on census forms, in court, and in government offices). Comparisons are often made with the status of Welsh and Scots Gaelic as a way of asserting that the British government is discriminating against Irish speakers, and by implication, all Irish people in Northern Ireland. Connections are also made with the issue of minority rights in a European context. Rights discourse is particularly strong in calls for parity of esteem, and in the process of elevating the Irish language to the position of litmus test for equality in recent political negotiations. It resonates with Irish speakers and many non–Irish speaking nationalists alike, making it a fairly powerful voice in current debates.

Rights discourse is also signalled by particular key words, concepts and arguments: 'rights,' 'civil rights' and 'human rights,' 'you can't hijack a language,' 'equality,' 'parity of esteem,' the responsibility of government to support minority cultures and uphold minority rights, and a denial that Irish can be wholly apolitical in the current sociopolitical context of Northern Ireland. Attempts are sometimes made to separate political allegiance from ethnic identity. And, importantly, the promotion of Irish is put above all other political and cultural considerations.

The following examples illustrate some of these characteristics. During a discussion of Sinn Féin's involvement with the Irish language, one man in his forties told me:

> I have a problem with people who *don't* run around and promote the language. To people who say Sinn Féin has hijacked the language, I'd say go *you* and hijack the language. But I wouldn't even accept the charge that they have. I would urge people who do think so to go and try to beat them at their own game.

The campaign to obtain funding for *Meánscoil Feirste* provides a number of good examples of rights discourse in practice. Although decolonizing discourse makes an appearance occasionally, and most advocates of cultural discourse would be quite supportive of the campaigns to obtain funding for Irish medium schools, rights discourse dominated the campaign and has been largely shaped by it. In late 1994, a press conference was held to announce the start of a 'pro–active campaign to highlight the anti–Irish sectarianism of the Department [of Education]' (*Irish News* 24–11–94). A key part of the campaign centred around the notion of parity of esteem for all traditions in Northern Ireland. A parent of one of the children attending the *Meánscoil* read a statement saying,

> Even the Department has had to admit that the school's record of achievement is second–to–none. We believe that the decision not to fund *Meánscoil Feirste* was in fact an attack on the whole idea of an independent Irish–medium secondary level sector to the education system here. It is also a clear signal to all concerned that the idea of equality and parity of esteem for all traditions has not yet been embraced by the British government.

Rights discourse both creates and is influenced by a different ideology about the Irish language, one which is neither apolitical nor narrowly attached to a single political perspective such as republicanism.

While the above descriptions of decolonizing discourse, cultural discourse and rights discourse demonstrate the range of perspectives on the Irish language held by nationalists, it is important also to look at how these discourses are used in real life. Below are two case studies which show how the different discourses, and the different ideological perspectives which they carry, can come into conflict with each other and sometimes be the source of misunderstanding.

Case study one:
Which discourse? The establishment of the ULTACH Trust

There was some controversy over the ULTACH Trust after its founding in 1989. Much of the debate was rooted in the belief, held by many Irish language activists in west Belfast, that the ULTACH Trust was advocating an 'apolitical' view of the Irish language. The presence of unionist politicians on the Board of Trustees; the special efforts made to attract, or at least to not alienate, unionists; the criticism made of those nationalists and republicans who, in the perception of the Trust, are using the language for their own political gains; and the type of discourse favoured by the Trust, suggest to many that the Trust is promoting the depoliticization of the Irish language. The result has been a considerable amount of suspicion on the part of some *Gaeilgeoirí*, and even outright hostility amongst a minority.

Critics of the ULTACH Trust can be loosely grouped into two camps, those who are suspicious of the very rationale behind the founding of the organization (usually, but not always, republicans), and those who welcome the founding of the Trust, but believe that it is flawed in some way. Members of Sinn Féin have expressed grave doubts about the motivations for the founding of the ULTACH Trust, drawing almost entirely on decolonizing discourse in their criticisms. They suggested it might be a government front, designed to regulate the Irish language revival by keeping control of its funding. Sinn Féin councillor and Irish language activist Máirtín Ó Muilleoir accused the government of having a deliberate policy designed to portray the Irish revival movement as sectarian, so that they could blame the decline of Irish on its association with nationalism rather than on their own policies. He suggests that that is the reason why funding for Irish has been tied to the Community Relations budget, rather than being treated separately as are Welsh and Scots Gaelic (*Lá* 5–8–93).

Derry Sinn Féin councillor Gearóid Ó hÉara wrote that having failed in their policy to oppress the Irish language, the British government needed a more clever policy *'leis na Paddies a choinneáil faoi smacht'* – 'to subjugate the Paddies' – and that the ULTACH Trust was part of that policy (*Lá* 5–8–93: 14). The republican newspaper *An Phoblacht* (20–2–92) accused the NIO of trying to buy off the Irish language vote by setting up the Community Relations Council and the ULTACH Trust, while at the same time cutting funding for the west Belfast group *Glór na nGael*. Republicans have also complained that there is no Sinn Féin (or even SDLP) representative on the Board of Trustees, in spite of the many dedicated Irish language activists associated with Sinn Féin and the work they have done on behalf of the language.

Criticisms from other quarters have focussed on perceived flaws in the organization, but tend to be somewhat milder in tone. An editorial in the *Andersonstown News* (6–4–91) gives a 'warm welcome' to an increase in funding for the Trust, but suggests that more money should be channelled into projects in west Belfast, where the bulk of language revival activities and organizations are located. Three years later in a regular Irish language column, it was suggested that the ULTACH Trust's money would be better spent on the Irish medium schools, since they are the heart of the movement and lacked government funding (*Andersonstown News* 21–5–94).[4]

Aside from disagreements on how the Trust's money should be spent, the most common criticisms are that the Board of Trustees is unbalanced or not representative of the nationalist side, and that they, too, use the Irish language for political ends. An article in Irish in the *Andersonstown News* (25–1–92) focussed on the latter point, although it is careful to temper its criticism by congratulating the Trust on its many accomplishments. The author softens the blow by suggesting that it would be dishonest not to raise the issue of problems which he or she sees with the Trust. The article then goes on to say that the first annual report of the Trust seems to side with the NIO on the issue of politicizing the language, because it says that some Irish language groups are alienating unionists by making it part of a nationalist political agenda. The article claims that this is inaccurate and insulting to Irish speakers, and asks for an explanation. It would be more fair, the article suggests, also to criticize the British government for using Irish as part of their efforts to entice nationalists away from Sinn Féin.

A more recent article written by Gearóid Ó Caireallán, the current president of the Gaelic League, addresses both the issue of the Board of Trustees being unbalanced and the politicization of the language (*Andersonstown News* 11–3–95: 24).

Ó Caireallán perceives a gap between the ULTACH Trust and the public caused in part by their political stance. He, too, criticizes the Trust for adopting the same stance as the NIO in opposition to Sinn Féin, suggesting that some members of the party are the most die–hard, diligent *Gaeilgeoirí* in the north. He argues that if there are unionist politicians on the Board of Trustees, it is only right that a Sinn Féin or nationalist political representative should also be on the board. This is the criticism of the ULTACH Trust which is, perhaps, the most disturbing to west Belfast Irish speakers. In its efforts to attract unionist support for the Irish language, some argue that the Trust is being unjust towards nationalists who are genuinely dedicated to the language.

A look at the ULTACH Trust's own materials gives a picture of the organization's views and how it wishes to portray itself. The first annual report of the ULTACH Trust was published in 1991. Under the heading 'Cross–Community Initiatives,' the Trust explains the emphasis put on the Protestant community:

> There appears to be an increase in interest in Irish among people from Protestant or unionist backgrounds ... However, it would be unwise to overestimate this trend, as the entire area is fraught with difficulties. Many unionists see Irish as being alien to their own tradition, and are deeply hostile to and distrustful of the language movement, which many of them see as having an essentially political agenda. The Trust's cross–community work is, and will be for some time, in the very delicate area of trying to overcome deep–seated prejudices. ...
>
> However, at present, the vast majority of language enthusiasts are nationalists, and, unfortunately, many of those nationalists fail to recognise that there can be any other rationale for involvement in the language movement. As a result, they often, despite themselves, make it difficult for interested unionists to learn the language.

> ... This problem arises from the fact that the cultural commitment of many Irish–speakers is inseparable from their political allegiance. Again, it should be emphasised that this is a perfectly justifiable ideological position: however, it is often accompanied by an assumption that unionists interested in Irish culture are well on the way to becoming nationalists. ... This unconscious ethnocentricity, rooted in an unresolved conflict between principles which claim to be non–political, and assumptions which are essentially political in their implications, is deeply ingrained in the Irish language movement (ULTACH Trust 1991: 8–10).

I have quoted this section of the first report at length to illustrate the effort made to achieve a careful balance between support for attracting unionists to the language (without offending distrustful unionists), and criticism of some nationalist attitudes (without alienating the majority in the revival movement). The report asserts that a nationalist position in relation to the language is legitimate, but at the same time it sees this as worrisome because such a position contains an element of unconscious ethnocentricity. This position has contributed to bad feelings on the part of some nationalists, as is evidenced by the comments mentioned above.

Aodán Mac Póilin, Director of the ULTACH Trust, is not unaware of the dilemma. He argues that for many, inclusive rhetoric about the language carries a different ideological subtext, one that in actuality excludes unionists. The Trust tries to make such inclusive rhetoric a reality, but this is not a simple task. As Mac Póilin sees it, a key problem lies in the weakness of Irish amongst the unionist population. This weakness means that the Trust must take positive action to promote Irish to Protestants. At the same time, the Trust is supposed to promote Irish throughout Northern Ireland to unionists and nationalists alike. While they must try to get unionists involved in the language, Mac Póilin emphasizes that the Trust has no right to undermine nationalist perceptions of the language. This dilemma has led Mac Póilin to seek an alternative to the political/apolitical dichotomy, which he attempts to do through the creative use of discourse and efforts to multipoliticize the language.

The ideology formulated in the quote above is similar to rights discourse in that it confirms the legitimacy of the association between the Irish language and nationalism, and it contains assertions that the language belongs to everybody, nationalist or unionist. It differs from most examples of rights discourse, however, in its criticisms of the position of some nationalists and in the special care taken to be balanced and fair. The first report does contain a sprinkling of cultural discourse as well:

> Not all Irish–language activists are well–meaning, and, for a highly vocal minority, the language is an integral part of apolitical programme. Sometimes it is in the interests of these groups to encourage unionist alienation from the language, and to identify Irish ever more closely with the nationalist community (ULTACH Trust 1991: 10).

In the ULTACH Trust's Second Report, published in 1994, the emphasis on increasing the language's cross community appeal is reiterated. It indicates a greater emphasis on Irish language education, from Irish medium schools and Irish as a school subject, to adult learning and the development of teaching materials. The new emphasis on funding Irish medium schools was due in part to the development of a capital fund, which gave the Trust greater freedom in the allocation of grants. The Second Report also seeks to define the Trust's philosophy more closely with regards to its cross community emphasis.

> The Trust has endeavoured to present the language and culture to the Protestant and unionist community in a way that will not be perceived as threatening their political identity. This process is sometimes described as the depoliticisation of the language: however, it is often more a process of creating the conditions through which Irish will become acceptable and accessible within all political traditions (ULTACH Trust 1994: 15).

This is in keeping with Mac Póilin's idea that the language

needs to be multipoliticized, rather than depoliticized. Still, the notion persists among many west Belfast *Gaeilgeoirí* that the Trust, amongst others, are attempting to depoliticize the language, and that this amounts to a threat to their own perceptions of the meaning of the Irish language and importance of Irish culture to their ethnic and political identities, since 'depoliticize' is often used as shorthand for denying the validity of a nationalist or republican perspective on the language.

A number of factors contribute to the persistence of the perception that the ULTACH Trust favours the ideology of depoliticization which is generally associated with cultural discourse. The 'hands–off' policy towards Sinn Féin and the Trust's association with the CCRU fosters suspicion among some nationalist *Gaeilgeoirí*, as demonstrated in the above discussion of attitudes towards the Trust. The relationship with the Cultural Traditions Group, strongly associated with cultural discourse and the community relations ethos, tends to colour perceptions of the Trust as well. The perception of open and eager support for Protestant interest in the language, combined with a perceived lack of support for language initiatives and organizations in Catholic areas, also fuels suspicions. Taken together, these particular perceptions give some people the general impression that the Trust favours the ideology of cultural discourse, in spite of what is explicitly stated in its official reports.

**Case study two:
Irish under attack? The *Glór na nGael* controversy**

Glór na nGael is the name of an annual all–Ireland competition to reward the community which has done the most to promote Irish in everyday life, a sort of Irish language 'tidy towns' competition. In 1982, the west Belfast committee of *Glór na nGael* was formed as an umbrella group for Irish language organizations to coordinate and facilitate entry into the competition, and to help promote the Irish language in Belfast.

West Belfast was awarded a number of the more minor prizes every year starting in 1982, and in 1986, 1990 and 1996 west Belfast won the most prestigious prize, the *Glór na nGael* trophy for the overall best area.

From its founding until its funding was withdrawn by the British government in 1990, *Glór na nGael* was involved in numerous activities. Initially the focus was on rights for Irish speakers, and the group was prominent in the bilingual street signs campaign of the 1980s as well as campaigns to increase the status of Irish in English medium schools, and for funding for Irish medium schools. Over the years, *Glór na nGael* has shifted its emphasis from campaigning to providing services for Irish speakers and learners. It holds Irish language classes in its own premises in west Belfast, and provides instructors for classes organized by other groups which are designed to attract both Protestants and Catholics, including classes and seminars in 'neutral' venues like the Ulster People's College (which is funded by the ULTACH Trust). *Glór* also provides support and teachers for the Irish medium nursery schools' movement, the organization's primary focus at the time funding was withdrawn.

In the months before the funding was withdrawn, there seemed little indication of the difficulties to come. The announcement that west Belfast had once again won first prize in the *Glór na nGael* competition came in March 1990. That same month, an editorial in the *Andersonstown News* (31–3–90) congratulated west Belfast *Glór na nGael* for the work they had done to 'bridge the gap' between Protestants and Catholics through the Irish language. At this stage, *Glór na nGael* had twenty Action for Community Employment (ACE) workers, most of whom worked in Irish medium nursery schools throughout the city. The money provided by the government to support these ACE workers constituted the bulk of the organization's funding, and allowed them to become involved in the community on a much wider scale than would have been possible with solely voluntary workers (although they did have a number of volunteers as well).

On 25 August 1990, without warning, the west Belfast office of *Glór na nGael* received a letter from the Northern Ireland Office stating that their funding under the ACE scheme had been withdrawn. No explanation was offered in the brief letter, but reference was made to a 1985 statement by then Secretary of State Douglas Hurd, in which he said that funds would not be made available to groups when that funding would 'have the effect of improving the standing and furthering the aims of a paramilitary organisation, whether directly or indirectly.' *Glór na nGael* was not the first community group to lose funding under the new policy of 'political vetting' – among others, the Twinbrook Tenants and Community Association (west Belfast), Conway Mill (west Belfast), the Mac Airt Centre in the Short Strand area of east Belfast, Dove House in Derry, and the Glencairn Community Association in Protestant west Belfast all had had their funding withdrawn over the period of time since the Hurd declaration.

The withdrawal of *Glór na nGael's* funding was immediately interpreted by west Belfast *Gaeilgeoirí* as an attack on the Irish language and on west Belfast as a whole. Many people were clearly shocked by the actions of the British government, coming as it did on the heels of the announcement that the government would be funding the newly established ULTACH Trust. One article in the *Andersonstown News* (1–9–90) listed a number of well–known and respected public figures who had recently sung the praises of *Glór na nGael* – including Minister for the *Gaeltacht* Pat 'The Cope' Ó Gallchóir, Bishop Cathal Daly, and Cardinal Tomás Ó Fiaich – as if to prove that the accusations against the organization were unfounded.

Seven of Belfast's eight Irish nursery schools, catering for approximately one hundred and forty children, were affected by the NIO ban which led to a cut in funding for *Glór na nGael*. None of the nurseries were receiving government funding of their own, so the loss of their *Glór na nGael* ACE workers was a severe blow. The schools were maintained through a variety of different fundraising drives, but the lack of ACE workers took its toll.

Within weeks of *Glór* receiving the news, a campaign to restore funding was launched, starting with a picket on the Training and Employment Agency which had paid the wages of the ACE workers, and a letter writing campaign to then Secretary of State Peter Brooke. *Glór na nGael's* ACE workers had been members of NUPE, the National Union of Public Employees, and the union also put their weight behind the campaign. *Glór* is also a member of NICVA, the Northern Ireland Council for Voluntary Action, which also protested against the policy of political vetting and came out in support of the organization. The committee of the Shaws Road nursery school accused Brooke of 'an attack on our culture and language,' and the Trustees of the ULTACH Trust took the unusual step of writing to Brooke asking him to reconsider his decision (*Andersonstown News* 15-9-90).

Speaking at a conference on censorship, the editor of *Lá*, Gearóid Ó Cairealláin, said 'Since the government withdrew funding from *Glór na nGael* there has been an increased awareness of how political vetting and censorship is used to control people's lives and culture' (*Andersonstown News* 20-10-90). A hard hitting editorial in the same paper strongly criticized the policy of political vetting as an attempt by the British to 'divide and conquer':

> *Glór na nGael* was targeted because the Stormont mandarins decided it didn't fit into the greater scheme of things. Unlike most other groups receiving community aid it was neither church–orientated nor middle of the road. ...
>
> Without the nationalist community the political vetting policy is in tatters. We are being asked to act as our own worst enemy – turning our backs on our neighbours because the Government decrees that they are unacceptable and unclean. We are to serve as a vetting body, screening our own community. Thus we can appear on the radio as long as we agree to the censorship of our

neighbours. We can receive grant–aid for community projects as long as we agree to use government buzzwords and adopt as Gospel government policy. ... (*Andersonstown News* 27–10–90)

The final sentence appears to be a veiled reference to the ULTACH Trust and the new government policy on the Irish language. 'Government buzzwords' seems to be a reference to certain aspects of cultural discourse, which has become increasingly important to the acquisition of funds for Irish language groups.

The accusation that the British government was using the Irish language to further its own ends was repeated in another editorial almost six months later. Commenting on an increase in funding for the ULTACH Trust, the editorial snipes:

> Certainly Brian Mawhinney's patronising claim yesterday that the money is designed to take the Irish language out of politics will be the cause of much mirth in the *Glór na nGael* offices. But then the parents of the eight nursery schools, run by *Glór na nGael* and denied funding since August last, know all about the Minister's determination to keep politics and the language separate – all politics that is except his own (*Andersonstown News* 6–4–91).

Clearly, resentment over the treatment of *Glór na nGael* reinforced some people's suspicions about the ULTACH Trust and increased mistrust of NIO motivations in funding the Irish language.

After a few months, the campaign to have funding restored was stepped up. A case of maladministration was taken up with the Northern Ireland Ombudsman, a petition to Peter Brooke was started, the *Dáil* was lobbied, and *Glór na nGael* offered to publish its accounts for all to see. Messages of support came in from many different quarters, from Labour's shadow Northern Ireland Secretary Kevin McNamara to Boston Mayor Ray Flynn. In December 1990 SDLP deputy leader Seamus Mallon tabled over twenty parliamentary questions on the issue. The British government, however, remained silent throughout the eighteen month campaign to regain funding, declining to comment when enquiries were made by journalists and refusing to give further details as to why funding was withdrawn.

An appeal for a review of the decision was made soon after the withdrawal of funding, but it was dismissed by the NIO without comment in October 1990. When *Glór na nGael* tried to gain access to documents regarding the NIO's decision to withdraw funding, their request was blocked by the issuing of a public immunity certificate. They then sought a judicial review in an effort to gain access to the documents, arguing that they could not defend themselves if they were not allowed to know the precise allegations which were being made against them. However, in a decision released in March 1991, the court decided against the case. In the end, *Glór na nGael* was never allowed access to any documents regarding their case, and no evidence was ever presented against them to support the allegations of paramilitary links.

Rumours, however, were rife. Some people believed that *Glór* was vetted because a prominent Irish language activist who is also a Sinn Féin councillor was a member of the committee up until a few months before funding was withdrawn. To counter this, it has been argued that this person was a founding member of the organization and active with the group since 1982, so why was ACE funding granted in the first place? Besides, since this person had left the committee before funding was withdrawn, why was *Glór na nGael's* appeal of the decision denied when the government must surely have been aware of this fact? If the involvement of people with republican sympathies was the problem, again, republicans had been involved in the founding of the organization. Rather than reflecting any strong republican sympathies in the Irish language movement, some people have suggested that this is because republicans are relatively 'thick on the ground' in west Belfast, so you are bound to find people with republican sympathies in almost any type of group or organization, from tenants' associations to church groups.

About the only evidence that could be mustered in support of the government's allegations against *Glór na nGael* came after funding had already been withdrawn. A former ACE worker with *Glór na nGael* who was once on the committee was later arrested and charged with paramilitary related offences. Not surprisingly, perhaps, this incident was downplayed and was not widely reported by the nationalist press. Labour's Kevin McNamara pointed out at the time that 'had all employers lost funding when staff were charged with criminal offences, the whole economy would grind to a halt, including the security forces' (*Irish News* 28–3–92). More importantly, perhaps, this person was not on the committee of *Glór* when funding was withdrawn, nor at the time of his arrest. None of the speculation about the alleged paramilitary links attributed to the committee of *Glór na nGael* seemed to offer a satisfactory explanation for the withdrawal of funding. For west Belfast *Gaeilgeoirí* who were familiar with the organization and friendly with the members of the committee, there was no logic and certainly no truth in the accusations.

Alternative explanations for the denial of funding were suggested by some of the more conspiratorially minded. Perhaps the NIO was less interested in alleged paramilitary links and more concerned with the threat that the Irish language movement posed to the British government. A series of high profile campaigns about the status of the Irish language in schools and funding for the burgeoning Irish medium education movement were embarrassing for the government, which was trying to promote a new image of equal respect for the 'two traditions' in Northern Ireland. According to this line of thought, the ULTACH Trust was established to prove the government's credentials in supporting the Irish language, and funding was removed from the less domesticated *Glór na nGael* to help bring the movement under control. Others saw it as a personal vendetta on the part of the former Minister for Education, Brian Mawhinney, who was attacked by *Glór na nGael* for his education proposals which would have reduced the status of the Irish language in secondary schools.

As the high profile campaign continued and gained increasing support at home and abroad, rumours surfaced that there were splits in the civil service over the decision to cut *Glór na nGael's* funding. Some people believe that those who made the decision were reprimanded for their handling of the situation. The Royal Ulster Constabulary continued to grant permission to *Glór* to make street collections during the period of the ban, perhaps indicating conflicting intelligence between the RUC and NIO sources. The sustained questioning and publicity was clearly becoming embarrassing for the NIO. The *Irish News* reported that a 'reliable source' told them that certain people were 'rapped hard over the knuckles because it was felt they had drastically underestimated the ensuing controversy' (28-3-92).

Whatever the reasons behind the NIO's decision to withdraw funding from *Glór na nGael*, it seriously heightened hostility towards the British government on the part of the Irish language movement, as well as fuelling suspicions of the ULTACH Trust. There was resentment at what was perceived by many to be an effort to rein in and control the movement, first through the manipulation of funding, and second by efforts to promote an 'acceptable' stance on the role of the Irish language in Northern Ireland. Increasingly, it seemed, there was an official line to toe when dealing with government agencies and funding bodies with regards to Irish. A certain discourse had to be used, particular 'buzzwords' employed, to get grants and official approval. The conciliatory 'feel good' language of cultural discourse has become increasingly favoured, although even this does not guarantee support. There was also resentment at what was perceived by some to be an effort to force the community to police itself and marginalize republicans. In the Irish language movement, as with many other community groups, this would mean shunning a number of important activists and in some cases, personal friends and colleagues.

The *Glór na nGael* controversy highlights a number of important issues. It clearly demonstrates the often antagonistic relationship which exists between large sections of the Irish language revival movement and the British government. It is also revealing in terms of *Glór na nGael's* place in the revival movement in west Belfast. For the most part, the movement closed ranks behind *Glór*, as did NUPE, NICVA, the ULTACH Trust and civil rights organizations such as the Centre for Research and Documentation (CRD) and the Committee on the Administration of Justice (CAJ) (*cf.* The Political Vetting of Community Work Working Group 1990). However, it also revealed some dissension, particularly on the issue of to what extent the Irish language movement should rely on, or become dependent upon, government funding.

The controversy also provides a glimpse into the struggle to define the meaning and importance of the Irish language to Irish identity and nationalist political aspirations. *Glór na nGael* used confrontational tactics in its campaigns to increase the profile of Irish and defend the status of the language in education. Although this was combined with seminars, Irish courses, publishing projects and more moderate politics as well, it was the confrontational aspects of their work which drew the attention of the NIO. As a grassroots organization in west Belfast, it became associated with nationalist politics, even though *Glór na nGael* made some of the first concerted efforts since the Troubles started to provide neutral access to Irish language classes in Belfast. In spite of these efforts, *Glór na nGael* did not conform to the more conciliatory two traditions/common heritage image which the British government wished to promote. In order for the Irish language to fit into the community relations project, its strongly nationalist and republican image had to be shed, or at least neutralized. The establishment of the ULTACH Trust and the acceptance of the CTG's interpretations of the significance of the Irish language were part of that project, as is the strategic use of funding to support groups and organizations that fit the desired image and ideology.

The British government policy of vetting 'undesirable' community organizations was officially shelved in 1995, but not before it had a profound effect on the Irish language revival movement. *Glór na nGael* regained its ACE funding in March 1992 after eighteen months of campaigning. No explanation was offered, other than the suggestion made by Peter Brooke that circumstances had 'changed significantly,' a suggestion which *Glór na nGael* denies, since the membership of the committee and the work of the organization had not changed since funding was withdrawn in 1990.

During the period of the campaign to restore funding, perhaps due in part to the *Glór na nGael* controversy, the ideology associated with cultural discourse made significant headway. It has become increasingly necessary and desirable to use this discourse, especially when dealing with government bodies, funding agencies and those 'outside' of the revival movement. At the same time, other discourses are still used in different situational contexts, and rights discourse still figures prominently in many campaigns.

Conclusion

The meanings associated with the Irish language in the nationalist community are not as straightforward as they are often portrayed. I have tried to show this by arguing that talk about the Irish language and the revival movement constitutes three discourses – decolonizing, cultural, and rights discourse. Not only do these competing discourses influence the differing ideologies and meanings associated with the language, they are the place where these meanings are created and debated. A certain amount of struggle and negotiation are still taking place as to which discourses, or which parts, will be most widely accepted. While cultural discourse is widely used and considered largely acceptable by most authorities, decolonizing discourse is now less common and is considered to be illegitimate by government authorities and unacceptable to many Irish speakers. Rights discourse is highly political but not necessarily republican, and is favoured by many Irish language activists and features strongly in many funding campaigns.

Each of the discourses is handled by institutions of authority in different ways. By incorporating aspects of cultural discourse into official or mainstream discourse on culture, tradition, and heritage, attempts have been made to neutralize the impact of decolonizing and rights discourses. Sometimes alternative discourses are suppressed, either directly (for example, removing funding from a controversial organization such as *Glór na nGael*), or indirectly (by attempting to delegitimize a particular discourse or certain aspects of it). There is also the option of simply ignoring an alternative discourse, hoping that it will lack the power, or that its users will lack the stamina, to press forward its ideological position.

The purpose of this essay is not to condemn or condone any of the views presented. Rather, I hope that this discussion will help to clarify some of the issues of debate regarding Irish in the north today, and to show that there is not one uniform nationalist position on the language. In her analysis of the Breton language, McDonald (1989) argues that there is no language external to the social context of its evaluation and use. This is nowhere more evident than in Northern Ireland. The variety of opinion on Irish language issues, nationalist, unionist and otherwise, should be seen as a good thing. It is my hope that open and informed debate, rather than doing harm, will help to strengthen the Irish language and its position in Northern Ireland as a whole.

References

Crozier, M. (ed.) 1989. *Cultural traditions in Northern Ireland: varieties of Irishness*. Proceedings of the Cultural Traditions Group Conference. Belfast: Queens University, Institute of Irish Studies.

_____. (ed.) 1990. *Cultural traditions in Northern Ireland: varieties of Britishness*. Proceedings of the Cultural Traditions Group Conference. Belfast: Queens University, Institute of Irish Studies.

Cultural Traditions Group. 1994. *Giving voices: the work of the Cultural Traditions Group 1990–1994*. Belfast: Community Relations Council.

Dunleavy, J. E. & G. W. Dunleavy, 1991. *Douglas Hyde: a maker of modern Ireland*. Oxford: University of California Press.

Fairclough, N. 1992. *Discourse and social change*. Cambridge: Polity Press.

Foucault, M. 1972. *The archaeology of knowledge*. London: Tavistock.

_____. 1982. The order of discourse. In *Language and politics* (ed.) M. Shapiro. Oxford: Blackwell.

Hutchinson, J. 1987. *The dynamics of cultural nationalism: the Gaelic revival and the creation of the Irish nation state*. London: Allen & Unwin.

Mac Póilin, A. 1989. *Presentation on the theme of cross–cultural connections*. Learning Links Communities, NICEA Conference, 24 June 1989. Unpublished.

McCoy, G. n.d. *Protestants and the Irish language in Northern Ireland*. Unpublished PhD thesis, Queens University of Belfast.

McDonald, M. 1989. *We are not French! language, culture and identity in Brittany*. London: Routledge.

Ó Fiaich, T. 1969. The language and political history. In *A view of the Irish language* (ed.) B. Ó Cuív. Dublin: The Stationary Office.

Ó Huallacháin, C. (Fr.) 1994. *The Irish and Irish: a sociolinguistic analysis of the relationship between a people and their language*. Dublin: Irish Franciscan Provincial Office.

The Political Vetting of Community Work Working Group 1990. *The political vetting of community work in Northern Ireland*. Belfast: Northern Ireland Council for Voluntary Action.

ULTACH Trust annual report/Iontaobhas ULTACH tuairisc bhliantúil1990–91. 1991. Belfast: ULTACH Trust.

ULTACH Trust: second report/Iontaobhas ULTACH: an dara tuairisc 1991–93. 1994. Belfast: ULTACH Trust.

Footnotes

1. First used around the time of the Downing Street Declaration, the term 'parity of esteem' was quickly adopted by Irish language activists, who saw the treatment of Irish as a sort of litmus test for its implementation.

2. In this case, the speaker is using 'military' to refer to the republican 'armed struggle' rather than the Irish or British army.

3. These terms carry a similar ambiguity when used in the context of other discourses. For example, the two traditions idea meshes well with the concept of parity of esteem and the assertion made by many nationalists that Irish is 'our own language.' On the other hand, the common heritage idea meshes with the widespread assertion made by many nationalists that the language belongs to both Protestants and Catholics. Aodán Mac Póilin of the ULTACH Trust argues that many nationalists do not think through the implications of this terminology. For example, he suggests that the term 'our own language' actively excludes non–Catholics and non–nationalists (Mac Póilin 1989; ULTACH Trust 1991).

4. Fifty per cent of the Trust's funding goes towards the support of Irish medium education.

Protestant Learners of Irish in Northern Ireland
GORDON McCOY

In recent years Protestant learners of Irish have become very 'mediagenic', attracting considerable interest in local newspapers, as well as in radio and television broadcasts. This interest is not without due reason. Protestant Irish speakers cross physical and ideological boundaries between the unionist and nationalist communities. They challenge the Catholic and/or nationalist image of the Irish language, as well as stereotypes of Northern Protestants as the champions of British culture in Ireland. The phenomenon of Protestant learners confronts many preconceived notions of what the Irish language represents; it also forces us to examine our attitudes to nationalism and unionism in Ireland.

In certain circumstances Protestant learners represent a religious minority within a minority language group. On the other hand, many of these Protestants would like to see a united Ireland, and by learning Irish they feel they are taking part in a nationalist project of cultural restoration. They are welcomed within Irish language circles, and their Protestantism seems unimportant and becomes backgrounded. Their opinions on the Irish language often differ little from their Catholic counterparts. Unionist learners of Irish are another case altogether. Their way of looking at the language often differs from that of nationalists, but they undercommunicate their views in Irish language circles for fear of giving offence. In preparing this chapter, I decided to concentrate on unionist learners of Irish as I wished to contribute something *new* to the understanding of the Irish language issue in Northern Ireland; the nationalist approach to Irish is comparatively well-known.

In this chapter I will draw upon the beliefs and experiences of 81 Protestant learners of Irish whom I studied for a doctoral thesis; most of the fieldwork was carried out between October

1992 and December 1994. I will use quotations and evidence supplied by many Protestant learners during 'one-off' interview situations. However, I will also mention two *groups* of learners which I studied over a period of time. Between February and October 1993 I taught Irish to a group of working-class Protestants in the Glencairn estate, which is in the Greater Shankill area of Belfast. I also observed a network of middle-class learners located in the affluent north Down region. The stark contrast between these two groups convinced me of the importance of class background in the analysis of Protestant learners of Irish.

Language and Identity

The dominant ideology embracing the Irish language is that of Irish nationalism; the language is connected with the desire to end British rule in Ireland. In the following quotation, a Protestant nationalist explains his interest in the language:

> I had a particular objection to the British Royal family, so I was exploring at the time my feelings about that and looking at the whole idea of the partition of the island of Ireland, and wondering why that had taken place, and I suppose over a period of years when I was at grammar school I started to think, 'Why is this island divided?' and I think I eventually came up with the idea that it shouldn't be... I sort of felt that there wasn't really a good reason for the island to be divided. I think from that knowledge I came round to saying,'Well, what are the features of Ireland, what are the essential aspects of its culture, and what are the things that people share, that wouldn't necessarily be too one-sided or the other, that wouldn't necessarily belong to one religious group or the other?' The biggest feature I could see then was the Irish language, and it was something that needn't necessarily belong to one group or the other.

This Irish speaker had discovered a secular symbol which he believed could be used to unite a people divided by religion. Many nationalist learners believe that the language provides a means by which they can express their Irish national and nationalist identities. Consequently, many nationalist Protestant learners do not understand how unionists can learn the language and retain their allegiance to Britain. This point is illustrated by the following quotations, which were supplied by three nationalist Irish speakers who were Protestant:

> Well, I find them a bit strange. I find it a bit strange to want to learn the language of a country and a people that you're trying to say you don't want to be a part of. Unionists say they want to be in Britain, they're saying the Irish language is part of their culture, so they should learn it, yet they're trying to keep themselves away from that culture as well.

> *GMc:* Can someone like Chris McGimpsey[1] who learns Irish be a unionist and an Irish speaker?
> *Learner:* Well, I don't think you could be, no, I don't think you could. But it's the beginning if they show an interest in Irish, it's something like, a wee bit like the thin end of the wedge. In a way they'll come to conclude, well, 'Irish isn't too bad at all and the Irish aren't too bad'. People who learn Irish have a leaning towards nationalism.

> I think it's a bit difficult when the government to which the unionists owe their allegiance has done so much to destroy the language over a period of time. If you get into the Irish language and that sort of thing, to a large extent that brings you closer to the Catholic people on this island. I think it brings you closer to them in a certain way and it encourages you to think in a more sort of Irish way and a more sort of all-island - it gives you an all-Ireland perspective on things and if you start to think, 'Well, this is my language, this is the language of the other people on this island'. I think it's a bit difficult to say, 'Well, what's this border doing here?'

In the first text the respondent cannot reconcile unionism and the Irish language. In the second text the speaker asserts that unionists who learn Irish do so because they are in the process of abandoning their allegiance to Britain. In the second and third texts the speakers articulate the belief that unionist learners will change their outlook when they are drawn into

Irish language circles. In the third text, the speaker claims that unionist Irish speakers cannot be loyal to successive British administrations which attempted to destroy the Irish language.

In the third text we have an example of linguistic determinism, the view that each language expresses and creates a distinct and autonomous system of thought. The belief that language and world-view are closely related has existed for centuries. Linguistic determinism is an important element of German Romantic nationalism, the Irish version of which linked the separatist movement to the revival of the Irish language. Since the Irish language is believed to be a repository of Irish nationality, advocates of linguistic determinism argue that unionists will acquire a nationalist outlook by learning the language.

The assertion that Protestants learn Irish because they are nationalist has some validity. The 1996 Social Attitudes Survey reported that no more than 6% of Protestants favour a united Ireland (Breen 1996: 36). However, 31% of my respondents said they were nationalist in outlook. Therefore the percentage of nationalists among the group I studied was higher than that among the Protestant population as a whole. However, the assertion that *all* Protestants learn Irish because they are nationalist is invalid; 46% of my respondents were unionist in outlook[2] . I must emphasise that these figures are not set in stone, as the proportion of unionist learners is rising.

It is true that many Protestants who learn Irish are nationalist in outlook. The idea that unionists can be converted to nationalism by means of the Irish language is more controversial; most of the nationalist learners I encountered had rejected unionism *before* they learned Irish. I have found little evidence of a 'conversion process' among unionist learners of Irish.

I asked some of my unionist respondents about their opinions on the relationship between the Irish language and Irish nationalism. In the course of one interview, a learner told me that he was afraid that his Protestant neighbours would intimidate him if they discovered his interest in Irish; they might believe that he was betraying the Protestant community. I asked him if Protestants who learned the Irish language *were* betraying their community, by becoming nationalist in their outlook, for example. He was most emphatic that they were not:

> That's totally nuts - absolutely not. I mean its quite the reverse, in fact, from my point of view. I'm pulling something out of a fire, you know, I'm not joining it in there. What I'm doing is redefining it as something that's important to me as an Ulster person. I want to learn Ulster Irish and its nothing to do with nationalism at all. I mean you'll be waiting for a long time before you'll find me coming round to that viewpoint... I'm going to pull it out from all the rubbish around it - all the nonsense.

This learner wishes to divest the Irish language of it's 'unnecessary' nationalist image, and views the language through unionist cultural lenses (for example, in his reference to Ulster Irish). A north Down learner explained the conflicting attitudes he held about the Irish language:

> I suppose there was a division between wanting to do it and being confronted by it, in the sense that you're kind of suspicious that to do it is some kind of political act, which you don't necessarily want to be part of... I never knew there was any neutral place that you could go to learn it, I mean any time that I met it, apart from hearing it on RTÉ, anytime that I met it was almost always in a political sense, you know, unless it was placenames, or you came across it in books. I mean I'm an historian, and I've come across it in history,you know, and I'd have to find translations of it, one was aware of its place, and all of that, and the literature as well. And I always wanted to be able to read the poetry... There was a division between wanting to do it and being confronted by it. It was a challenge to learn it, but at the same time the republican tradition of it was screaming at me and there was the oppressive connotations of it in the South.

This unionist learner struggles with his wish to enhance his knowledge of Irish culture and his dislike of the association of the Irish language with nationalism. His account illustrates the ambivalent feelings many unionist learners have about Irish. They perceive the ideological gulf that lies between themselves and nationalist Irish speakers to be a large one. In the following text, the speaker discusses a magazine supplement about 'raving nationalist' Irish speakers who were Protestant:

> I've no doubt that they were very sincere people, but I think maybe because I think, 'Oh. isn't that funny, that person's Protestant and yet very much a nationalist'. But the fact of the matter is that when I'm viewing it from my standpoint as an Ulster Protestant, it's completely sort of - it's very unusual for any of us to suddenly turn and become an Irish nationalist, because it's exactly the opposite of what you are. For me to turn round and suddenly become a nationalist would be very odd, and you would wonder where that person was coming from to think like that.

Just as many nationalists cannot understand how unionists can learn Irish and retain their political allegiances, this text reveals the incredulity of the speaker at the suggestion that she may become a nationalist.

Unionist learners do not feel that they must choose between two mutually opposed British and Irish cultures. Rather, they often express a syncretic cultural identity which draws upon elements of Britishness and Irishness:

> I feel quite privileged now because I mean you feel the best of both worlds. You extract from both sides what you like best, you know. I haven't come to terms with anything now really. I'm happy to be British-Irish or Irish-British or whatever, you can take pleasure from both. I mean, I take great pleasure in looking at the 'Changing of the Guard' or something like that there ... It doesn't mean to say that I can take no pleasure in things that I took pleasure in before. I mean, when they play 'The Land of Hope and Glory' or something, it doesn't mean to say that I shouldn't, I feel quite happy to associate with that, and I've no problems about it. I'd say that the Irish culture would certainly be part of me now, yes, sure, and I'm a better person for it.

This north Down learner is adamant that she is not embracing an Irish nationalist identity at the expense of her British one; the way in which her response is worded suggests that she might have felt that this was expected of her.

For many Protestants, national identity is situational and complex (Waddell and Cairns 1986). Protestants may feel Irish on holiday in Donegal, British on Remembrance Day, and subscribe to an Ulster identity when they feel that the British government has failed them. Middle-class unionists often express a sense of Irishness (albeit a vague and ill-defined one) in cultural or geographical terms. They may articulate Irish identities by supporting the Irish rugby team or Irish athletes at the Olympic games. They will also take holidays in the Republic of Ireland, thereby familiarising themselves with other parts of Ireland (Todd 1987: 16). Unionist intellectuals often favour the expression of an Irish identity which is compatible with a British one (e.g. Foster 1995). The Irish language provides a means for some unionists to express an Irish identity which they feel is harmonious with their allegiance to Britain.

Working-class unionists are more attracted to an Ulster national identity than their middle-class counterparts. This identity has as its primary imagined community Northern Protestants, while there is a secondary identification with Britain (Todd 1987: 3). Moxon-Browne explains the Ulster allegiance in terms of disillusionment with English policy in Northern Ireland (1991: 28). Working-class unionists who learn Irish may associate the language with this identity, expressing a preference for the Ulster dialect of the language:

> If someone says to me, 'What's the Irish for that?', I'll be able to say that in Irish and that's that. And I regard myself in a sense as Irish in that I regard myself as an Ulsterman and as part of the island. It's everything else that I am not terribly happy with - the way we have been treated by Britain. And I think if you're going to establish an identity for yourself I would say, 'I'm a Christian first', and then I would say, 'I'm an Ulsterman, and as an Ulsterman I'm Irish', and it doesn't mean that I want to be involved with the Republic in any sense, but it does mean that I'm

from the island of Ireland and perhaps there's a degree of learning identity in learning Irish... Speaking Irish is not a republican thing to do, its an Ulster thing to do, and to speak in the Ulster language and to speak Gaelic in Ulster is a thing that Ulstermen should do. I'd like to see them all speaking in Irish.

In this text the speaker alternates between expressing Irish and Ulster identifications. Towards the end of the text the speaker uses the term 'Gaelic', thus challenging the insular image of the language by introducing a semantic link to Scottish Gaelic.

Nationalists who believe that unionists will lose their political outlook when they socialise with Irish speakers are often mistaken. Many Protestants, especially middle-class ones, have Catholic friends and take holidays in the Republic of Ireland, but they do not adopt the views of the nationalists they encounter. Furthermore, the nationalist belief that unionists would abandon their political allegiances upon their exposure to Irish history is optimistic, to say the least. History is a product of present concerns as well as a storehouse of essential truths. Thus there are unionist and nationalist *histories* of the Irish language:

> I would come from the unionist tradition, and I could actually use my knowledge of Irish at the moment to defend the unionist position an awful lot better than most of the unionists ... the absurdity of Ireland as a sort of Gaelic, Catholic nation and the idea that because the sea is round it that makes it a nation. The language links us with Scotland and with Wales and with Cornwall, and actually England too. England is as Celtic a nation as we are. So I would see the Irish language as linking us with the other Celtic peoples, and I think its a blind spot, this obsession with England as an enemy. The English are the same people as we are, so it seems to me that Irish language is something which holds the British Isles together. I mean the very word 'British' speaks to me of a Celtic language, you know, and not of English. Old Shakespeare with his England and her sister nations bound together by the triumph of sea. I see the sea as binding nations together. The sea has always bound Kintyre and County Antrim, and for these absurd people to draw a line down there and say,

'This is Ireland and that is Scotland' - that's rubbish.

By describing Irish as a Celtic language, this learner symbolically links the language to the British 'mainland'. He rejects what he perceives to be the attempt of Irish nationalism to substitute an insular Irish identity for one embracing the historical links between Britain and Ireland. His reference to the sea 'binding nations together' echoes the unionist assertion that the Irish Sea facilitated rather than hindered population movements between Britain and Ireland in ancient times.

It is not only nationalist Irish speakers who hope that the language can be used to change the opinions of others. Many middle-class unionist learners believe that working-class learners would adopt their liberal views if they learn Irish:

> This language was here before any of this conflict between Protestant and Catholic. I think that's something that would do an awful lot for the advance of this country and the advance of community relations, if Protestants became more aware of the cultural heritage that they share with their Catholic neighbours ... And they lack a real cultural heritage, this nonsense of beating Lambeg drums on the 'Twelfth', really, it's a bit shallow. They've got something a lot more rich than that. I was trying to tap into that on my own as well, learning Irish ... I would like to see some kind of attempt to raise the awareness among the Protestant people of the cultural awareness that they share with everybody on this island, instead of saying 'no' to everything that doesn't wear an orange and purple sash, which is really what it's become.

This middle-class unionist balances his positive opinion of the Irish language with a negative evaluation of Protestant working-class Orange culture. The speaker wishes to replace and/or supplement Orange culture with Irish culture. Middle-class unionist learners, like the person I have just quoted, believe that working-class loyalists will become less anti-Catholic if they learn Irish.

I doubt the 'conversion' of unionists to nationalism or even liberal unionism by means of the Irish language. However,

Protestants make many exciting discoveries when they take an interest in the Irish language. They often acquire a new way of looking at their surroundings. Many learners describe their interest in the Irish language as one that comes to have enormous personal benefit for them:

> I remember when we first started, I found a real buzz with, do you know it was like lifting, *breaking through silence* or something because I was really going, 'This is something I *never ever* knew'. And if I heard Irish, I didn't know what it meant, but then, it was sort of like, the cloud lifting or something and I realised, 'This is *the* language', and I thought, 'Why on earth didn't I do this earlier in my life?'

In the following text, a learner describes her experiences in an Irish language college in Donegal:

> Every night the college organised something ... And a fiddler, and of course the famous Lillis (Lillis Ó Laoire, a singer from Donegal), the *sean-nós* singer, he was there, and then we'd a dinner one night and a *céilí*, and then afterwards you went to Biddy's (a local bar). But every afternoon there was a programme as well. You could have gone hill-walking, if you'd any interest in playing an instrument, you had that, and the famous *sean-nós* singing which I adored ... I mean it was 'now for something completely different'. I have never seen anything like that in my life. I had never heard anything like it. I didn't know those things existed. I'd never been to a *céilí*, and everything was a revelation ... (after listening to Lillis Ó Laoire talking about traditional songs) Really, he could have been speaking any language, but it was beautiful you know, it really sounded beautiful, though I didn't understand it.

Many adult Protestant learners experience a tremendous sense of excitement when they begin to learn Irish, but they also feel a sense of regret that they were not informed about the language earlier in their lives. Graduates often told me they would have chosen to study Irish at degree level had they been more aware of the language before they enrolled for university. Among Protestant learners there was an almost universal regret that the language had not been introduced to them during their school years.

Some Protestant learners have difficulty in identifying with the Irish language because their interest receives little support in their own community:

> I find it strange, because a part of me says, 'Well you're here and you live in this land and it should be part of you', but in a sense at the same token, my background isn't, and therefore it nearly feels that it would always be an 'add on'... It's nearly like learning a foreign language, it's nearly like that, yeah. I would like to feel that I own an Irish culture. I would like to establish it as part of my - but I don't see it in my family background and therefore it's difficult. In my own circle of friends and family and stuff, it wouldn't be really encouraged, or they wouldn't appreciate it fully, so it's not something that I'm actually going back to, what I feel to be my roots or something ... I wouldn't want to be narrow, I mean, exclude friendships (with Catholics/Irish speakers) across the board, or whatever, you know. I'd quite like that, it's just circumstances, and where I live, and *everything*, and work. It just reinforces the circle that I'm in, and there isn't the opportunities, really. Unless the (Irish) class, the likes of the class forces a mix and a broadening, and a changing over, it's forced a change in that sense. Whether it continues, I think it would need to be a conscious effort on my part which might be difficult on a long term basis. I don't know.

The degree to which learners can identify with Irish depends upon the knowledge that is available to them. The speaker in the above text had just begun to learn Irish. She struggles to identify with the Irish language, but feels she cannot as it is not part of her background. When I had finished interviewing this learner, I attempted to demonstrate to her that there was a tradition of Protestant Irish speakers. I did this by showing her a Protestant translation of the New Testament into Irish, whereupon she became tremendously excited, exclaiming, 'Why did no-one show me this before? Why did no-one tell me about this?'

Many Protestant learners lessen their alienation from Irish by drawing upon historical evidence of previous Protestant involvement in the language. This Gaelic past enables contemporary Protestants to 'traditionalise' their interest in Irish:

> Well, its programmes like that, its programmes like the McAdam programme (a BBC production on the life of Robert McAdam, a nineteenth-century antiquarian and revivalist), and the other articles I've read. All of that makes one feel that you're actually part of a tradition, you know, not breaking into a tradition, not sticking out like a sore thumb... I didn't even know, for instance, that there had been Presbyterian speakers of Gaelic in County Down. You know, things I discovered like that. I discovered that in my own school that Neilson (a nineteenth-century Presbyterian minister and scholar of the Irish language) had taught there and everything. Well, all these things, well, they didn't make any difference to me learning the thing, but there was a way in which you felt a lot more confident. I suppose I felt that I wasn't some kind of lunatic eccentric, you know.

In this text a north Down learner associates the Irish language with a Protestant heritage (the McAdam programme and the articles), his school tradition (William Neilson), and his local identity (County Down). These have the combined effect of rationalising his interest in Irish in terms of a tradition. Even if there are not many contemporary Protestant learners of Irish with whom he can identify, he feels re-assured that many other Protestants spoke Irish in the past. In this way, the learner circumvents occasional feelings of isolation among Catholic Irish speakers.

Other Identities

When considering the Irish language, commentators often concentrate on the ideologies of nationalism and unionism, as well as features of Protestantism and Catholicism in Ireland. It is important to consider that learners of Irish often have other kinds of identification; local community and familial identities, for example. In many situations these 'small-scale' identities may be more important to learners of Irish than 'macro-level' national or religious ones. In the following quotation, the speaker is replying to the question, 'When did you first want to learn Irish?'

> Why, I was hoping no-one would ask me that! I don't know why I'm learning Irish. I've always been fascinated with words and the crazy spelling. My father had Irish - the only thing that I remember him saying was *'Cad é mar atá tú?'* ('How are you?'). And then of course on holiday in Bunbeag (in North Donegal). I was there three times a year, four times a year ... I always went to it, and now looking back, I know it was Gaeltacht, but then we didn't know, but we heard the language and we saw the writing, and I remember falling madly in love with the word *'aisling'* (vision), and calling my house that ... and the names used to fascinate me on the signs.

This north Down learner attributes her interest in Irish to her family history, her childhood experiences, as well her fascination with language. She and the other members of the group relate their interest in Irish to long-established customs in the district, including traditional music and dancing. The group also read about the Protestant Gaelic tradition in County Down and are enthusiastic about the Irish roots of local surnames and placenames. The group feels that Irish culture has not been 'imported' from other parts of Ireland, but represents part of the tradition of their local community. While discussing the Irish language with the north Down learners, I formed the impression that their local community identity was as relevant to them as wider and more abstract concepts of British and Irish identity.

Thus small-scale affiliations are important when Irish speakers consider their relationship with the language. On the other hand, western concepts of ethnicity and culture that transcend national boundaries have had their influence on Irish language enthusiasts. Both Protestant and Catholic learners of

Irish are influenced by a global upsurge of interest in minority cultures and languages. This is particularly true of younger learners of Irish; it is now trendy to be 'trad':

> *GMc.:* What do your friends think of your interest in Irish?
> *Learner:* They'd say, 'That's very fashionable of you.' I think Irish *is* fashionable, actually. I think its fashionable to pick up on anything that's sort of like - because everyone thinks, oh, isn't it sad that the native Americans are being trampled on, let's make them a reserve for them all to live in. And it's the same with languages and folk art and so on, and all that sort of stuff. There's a sort of desire to protect it, and it's a bit *trendy*, really. It's because the modern world is so homogenised, you go to any country in the world and you'll be able to buy a tin of Coke and Kentucky Fried Chicken. Everything is the same now, getting to be the same. So anything that's old and definitely more part of one country is interesting and makes the world a more interesting place. That's why Belfast is crammed with all these little shops selling wooden ornaments and beads from the Third World.

The Irish language is related to the world-wide upsurge of interest in minority ethnicity and the dislike of bland, homogenous Anglo-American culture. As such, Irish is de-ethnicised by divorcing it from concepts of Catholicism and nationalism; the language is represented as part of a culture that is accessible to everyone.

Protestant Learners and the Irish Language 'Scene'

I have shown how nationalists, including Protestant ones, regard the connection between the Irish language and Irish nationalism as common-sensical and natural. However, unionists who learn the Irish language do not accept certain conventions of the Irish language scene. This leads to cultural mis-matches between unionist and nationalist Irish speakers. The following incident happened during a cross-community Irish language class. The teacher handed out a photocopied song that is very popular among Irish speakers; the song includes a line which refers to driving the '*na Gaill*' (the foreigners) out of Ireland[3]. One unionist learner reacted in this way:

> That song that we did, I didn't feel too happy about singing it. I must admit, I really didn't. You see, I think that's from her (the teacher's) background, you know, it's acceptable, but it does feel odd ... And funny enough, there was a week's lapse, and Cathal gave me a lift home, and *he* actually brought it up that he didn't feel right in singing it either, and he felt it was out of place in a mixed group ... and I appreciated that someone from a Roman Catholic background had differing opinions or whatever, would feel the same about it.

Unionist learners object to aspects of the Irish language scene, such as singing republican songs (usually in English!), and discussions about the GAA, in which few Protestants express an interest. Like the learner quoted above, most unionist learners of Irish keep a very low profile at Irish language classes and events. They are fearful of objecting to certain conventions as they feel at times that they are observing a culture which is alien to them. The fact that nationalist Irish speakers are unaware when they are giving offence compounds the problem.

As the Irish language is often associated with the Catholic community, Protestant learners of Irish find that they are often assumed to be Catholic. This often irritates them as it underlines their distinctiveness from other Irish speakers. In the following text 'Adele', who was brought up on the Shankill Road, tells her experiences to myself and 'Ruth', a fellow Protestant learner. Adele begins by relating an incident which occurred while she was attending an Irish language course in Donegal:

> There was this German girl in our class called Frederika, and she bounced up to me one day and said, 'Oh, you're from Belfast' and I said, 'Yes' and she said, 'Oh, do you know the *Cultúrlann*' and I said, 'Yes, I do, I've been there once or twice', and she said, 'Oh, I love it' and then she started listing all these people (mentions the

names of members of the language movement), did I know them, all the usual ones and I said, 'Well, I didn't know them personally, but I know who they are'. And she just showed a lack of understanding of the issues involved, you know, it was kind of like you know, 'You're into Irish, therefore you must be a sort of republican Falls Road kind of person'...

And then the *pièce de résistance* came on the second day of the course. In the coffee break I was talking to this American woman, and Frederika was there, and the American said to Frederika, 'Oh do you come to Ireland often?' and Frederika said, 'Yes, I come at least once a year', and all this. And she said, 'I've been to Belfast and I love Belfast, people are so wonderful, and it's great. But the people on the Shankill Road, they're just horrible! They're just such horrible people! One day I went for a walk up the Shankill Road and the people were so horrible and it was just like a slum, you know and everything was so dirty.' And she just went on like this, and I just stood there, and I have to say I felt like a ton weight had come down on my head, you know, I just stood there thinking, 'What is the point of going on with this, this constant battle, you're always on the outside ...

I was saying to Margaret (a friend who was learning Irish), you know, like some other classes I've been to in the Arts Club and the Ulster People's College (Irish classes in south Belfast)... I always felt a wee bit on edge, not massively so, but just enough to make you that wee bit uncomfortable, and everybody would get in with the teacher, but *you* wouldn't be in. You'd always be hanging about sort of not quite knowing what to do. Even at the Ulster People's College, until *you* sort of came (addresses Ruth) I really just came and then went home ...

Seán (a teacher at the Donegal course) initiated this discussion about the language, 'Did we think it was dying, did we think it was worth reviving and all this'. And I just sat there thinking, you know, Seán and all the others were quoting things that were good, like the *Cultúrlann*, all the newspapers like *Lá*, but I just sort of thought, 'All the things that were quoted were all things that were in west Belfast or you know, your average Protestant, even a liberal Protestant, would feel a bit uncomfortable about'. And I just sat there and I just sort of wanted to say 'Look, you know, this is all very well, but what about me? What about me and my friends and people like me? We are human beings, we are here in front of you. How do we get included in all of this? It's like we don't exist'.

In this text Adele indicates her reluctance to travel to Catholic west Belfast and her lack of identification with the language revival there. The *pièce de résistance* comes when a foreigner, whom she expected to be more neutral in outlook, expresses anti-Protestant attitudes. In doing so, she makes a terrible *faux pas* in terms of the social etiquette in Northern Ireland, but Adele decides that she cannot embarrass Frederika by telling her that she is speaking to a Shankill Protestant; thus she draws upon a convention which prohibits embarrassing her interlocutor. Adele's decision does not challenge Frederika's belief that all 'indigenous' learners of Irish are Catholic.

When I talked to Adele on another occasion, she expanded the events related above to elaborate on what she called the 'Catholic tribalism' of Irish speakers. She said that they discuss life in their home districts, arrange to socialise in areas where Protestants are reluctant to go, and discuss GAA matches that Protestants have little interest in. In doing so, Catholic Irish speakers create and sustain friendships that are restricted to other Catholics. They draw upon 'pools of predictability' of shared background and experience which facilitate intra-Catholic socialisation (Burton 1978: 65). In such encounters Adele's distinctive Protestant identity is highlighted, although she is a 'fellow' nationalist.

Protestant learners who suspect that their religious or political affiliations may be resented by Catholic learners often attempt to conceal their religious identities from other Irish speakers. For example, one learner told me that Catholics on a Gaeltacht course stare at her when she tells them that she is from Bangor (which implies that she is a Protestant). She prefers to tell other Irish speakers that she is from County Down (which gives no indication of her religious affiliation). Other Protestants go further and deliberately masquerade as Catholics when they believe that they may be in danger if their real identities are revealed. One Protestant, who learned Irish in west Belfast, bought a copy of the *Andersonstown News* every week in order to be able to pose as a local in class.

Adele's experiences represent a type of 'worse-case scenario' that Protestants relate about their interaction with Catholic Irish speakers. Protestant learners feel a sense of difference between themselves and Catholic Irish speakers, but the potential to form lifelong friendships with Catholics exists. In many instances the shared love of the Irish language overcomes political and sectarian divisions. In the following text, a learner describes his experience of learning Irish in an evening class run by the nationalist-controlled Queen's University Students' Union:

> I find that one of the great things about it is, I think it actually creates more trust than anything else, especially with young Catholics who are turning against the Church so fast. But it is such a loaded thing, and it has become such a loaded thing, that I find that it breaks down barriers very quickly. When you know Catholics who don't speak Irish at all, the fact that you know it sort of makes them look at you in a much more sympathetic, not sympathetic, but a more trusting way. I find it breaks down barriers that way ...
>
> (on going to the class at Queen's University) I was a bit sort of nervy about going, because it was a sort of bad time in the 'troubles', and I thought, 'I'm going to be swamped by this, you know. I'll have to sit putting up with all sorts of stuff.' And in fact consistently I've found that in most Irish language circles they don't care what you are as long as you speak Irish, the love of Irish predominates over everything, and I found the reverse in fact. In fact, one of the other reasons why I was let off with not doing my irregular verbs was I quite often had 'wee pet status'. But I never found, augh, well occasionally in the bar afterwards, when I was talking English to people, you'd have a discussion that would get a wee bit fraught. But I never had any problem, you know.

In this text the speaker asserts that increasing secularism dissolves tensions between Irish speakers from differing religious backgrounds. Political issues arise when the class has finished and its organisers no longer have any control over the issues that will be discussed. The speaker even claims that as a Protestant he is especially welcomed within an Irish language environment. In the following text, a unionist university student explains how he related to classmates that did not share his political views while on a Gaeltacht course:

> There was a couple of bitter rows with people who were real hard-liners, but most of us got through it with humour. There was a lot of humour between us and we ignored the subject and said it was really a matter of 'You have your idea, I have mine, like, you know, just leave it aside'... When I was in the Gaeltacht I made some very close friends among some of those students and the political issue just fell aside. And we're still very close friends, although if you asked us about our political beliefs, they were completely different ... The Gaeltacht just intensified the ones who were friends and the ones who were just acquaintances.

In forming friendships, the speaker and his Catholic friends decided to avoid political issues in conversation, as they would not agree about them. They followed the rules for 'mixed' socialisation in Northern Ireland by avoiding contentious issues. As such, they agreed to undercommunicate aspects of their ethnic identities. Humour was used to avert conflict between the students; this is a stylistic device often employed to defuse tense situations (Tannen 1989).

Learners of Irish sense a degree of autonomy of the language movement from nationalism. They also notice that their teachers make great efforts to make them feel welcome. Members of the Irish language movement wish to welcome Protestant learners of Irish for many reasons: Catholics regard themselves as being less sectarian than Protestants; the Irish language movement is avowedly non-sectarian, and some Irish speakers strive to put this principle into practice; nationalist Irish-speakers believe that to deny Protestants access to the Irish language would symbolically bar them from admittance to the Irish nation; and Irish speakers are keen to encourage others to take an interest in a language which they fear is in danger of becoming extinct.

When Protestant and Catholic speakers of Irish meet for the first time, they often follow the social etiquette which entails the avoidance of religious and political topics of conversation. However, Protestant learners often notice that many Catholic Irish speakers depart from this etiquette, as they feel the need to prove they are not republican. Thus Protestant learners often become the unwitting confidantes of Catholic Irish speakers who bitterly resent the republican image of the Irish language. This process is often two-way; many Protestant learners, especially middle-class ones, feel they must distance themselves from the loyalist extremists of their own community. As one learner explained to me, 'We need to prove that we're not Orange bigots and they have to prove they're not Provos'.

In the absence of such 'proof', Protestant and Catholic Irish speakers often fantasise about each other's political beliefs, leading to incidents which reveal mutual misunderstandings. The experience of a Protestant friend of mine provides an unfortunate illustration of this phenomenon. While studying the Irish language at university, he was disturbed by 'jokes' about his being a spy for MI5. Upon finishing the course, he continued his involvement in the Irish language scene, but noticed that some members of the Irish language movement fell silent when he was near them. Later he moved to Scotland and became involved in the Gaelic language and music scene. He told me that he felt more at home in this environment, as the political and sectarian barriers which prevented him from being comfortable in the Irish language scene did not exist in Gaelic Scotland.

Finding a Class

At present most Irish language classes in Northern Ireland are in nationalist districts. Protestants, including many nationalist ones, are often reluctant to go into these areas for many reasons: they are afraid of republicans, as they fear being mistaken for loyalist or security force spies; they may have jobs, such as those in the civil service, that identify them with the British state; they may abhor violence, and those who support it; some of them fear being shunned by Irish speakers; they may object to a nationalist and/or republican bias in the teaching of Irish; and in the case of west Belfast, they are afraid of losing their cars to joyriders. Many Protestant learners do not go into nationalist districts to learn Irish because they simply do not know what to expect there; as one put it to me, 'I'd be a stranger in a strange land'.

Some Protestants feel uncomfortable at the prospect of attending classes located in nationalist districts, even if they feel they would be made welcome there. One north Down learner told me that he had attended a couple of classes in *Cumann Chluain Ard*, an Irish language society in west Belfast, but that he wouldn't go there often:

> *GMc.:* So, would you go back to it?
> *Learner:* Oh aye, I would. I wouldn't go regularly, but, because I would be doubtful about the politics of some of the people who went there. Whereas I may be nationalist, I am certainly not in any sense republican in the normal sort of meaning of that word, locally, or any way in favour of violence.

In another conversation this learner told me he would not go to the Shankill Road to learn Irish; although he would be a Protestant in a Protestant district, there would be people in a class there who would support violence to achieve their political goals. In his social activities, the support or non-support for violence is a more important factor for the learner than the ideologies of unionism and nationalism. Thus he feels more comfortable in the presence of non-violent unionists than fellow nationalists who support violence to achieve a united Ireland. This 'non-violence' criteria for comfortable social interaction is a feature of the north Down group as a whole; the learners often castigate both republican and loyalist 'extremists'. I can generalise from these experiences by saying that middle-class Catholic and Protestant learners often get along together because they are opposed to the use of force to achieve political goals in Northern Ireland.

In the following text, a nationalist learner from east Belfast voices her fears about travelling to nationalist *districts* of the city to learn Irish:

> I'd wanted to do it for the last few years, but I was always a bit shy of doing it because I don't know where the impression came from, but I had the impression that I would really have to go into quite nationalist areas to learn it, and I was a bit scared of that. So it was a relief when I heard that the YM (the YMCA has premises in Belfast city-centre) has offered courses and that was sort of open, neutral territory, if you like. It's awful to be influenced in that way, but I feel it was somewhere I could learn the language, I wouldn't be under pressure, I wouldn't be feeling that everybody would be watching me or I wouldn't be on my guard, that sort of thing.

Such classes are at a very early and precarious stage of development. Furthermore, Protestant learners are often unaware of the number of Irish classes in 'safe' areas that are available to them. Classes in neutral or Protestant districts often cater for complete beginners, and there are few support mechanisms for those Protestants who get past the beginners' or intermediate learners' stage. If inter-communal conflict increases, classes in Protestant districts often close, due to local hostility or the fear of it.

Many Protestant learners like to go to the Gaeltacht to learn Irish as they feel more comfortable with Irish speakers from the Republic of Ireland. The image of the Irish language in the Republic differs from that in Northern Ireland. As the Southern state settled down in the years after partition, nationalist fervour declined. Public opinion was not favourable towards the Irish language movement, which was seen as 'excessively nationalistic, even xenophobic', associating Irishness with 'militant and narrow Catholicism' (Tovey et al. 1989: 32).

Membership of the European Union encourages notions of diversity and plurality, and a 'movement beyond narrow homogenising nationalism' (Todd 1994: 156). Today young enthusiasts are attempting to give the language a modern and 'trendy' image, replacing the isolationist ideology embracing Irish with one which incorporates pluralist and secular beliefs. Attempts are being made to define an image for Irish which rejects the associations of the language with the Catholic Church and republicanism. Protestant learners of Irish respond favourably to these moves, and often feel more relaxed in learning venues across the border:

> It's quite clear to me that the language is far more important than political issues to them. Certainly any of the other teachers that I've come across there haven't been any with real interest in the politics of Northern Ireland anyway.

> Whenever you go over the border, you just sort of - it's so - you know, you just feel this cloud lifting, like you've shed this burden or something, you know, and it's so relaxed and people don't have the same problems.

Community Pressure on Protestant Learners

I have related how some Protestant Irish speakers have good relations with their Catholic counterparts. In fact, some of them told me they would be more afraid of 'their own' than Irish-speaking Catholics. Protestant learners living in working-class districts are afraid that their interest in Irish will be discovered by 'hoods' or paramilitaries who may intimidate them. Some of them feel they cannot go to classes even if they are made available in their own districts; they prefer to travel anonymously to other areas in order to learn Irish.

Protestants whose unionism is beyond doubt, such as loyalist paramilitaries, have no problem with telling working-class Protestants that they are learning Irish; their loyalty to their community is beyond doubt. Ian Adamson, a Belfast councillor interested in the Irish language, related a telling incident to me[4]. Before the 'troubles', in the late 1960s, he was a medical student living in the Sandy Row area:

> When I went to Sandy Row I brought a lot of my books, the Irish Texts Society and all my Gaelic books. I have a complete set of the Irish Texts Society and the *Annals of Ulster* ... I'd all these books and a wee lady down the street, she came in to see if she could do for me, and look after me, and I said that would be great. But whenever word got about the place about all these strange books, almost like devil worship, people gave me funny looks, you know. They didn't talk to me. So I went to Smithfield (market) because that's where I always bought everything. I bought this big picture of the Queen, and I put it up on the mantelpiece such that you could see it when you passed the window, and it just (clicks fingers) changed like that - the whole attitude. So I never had any trouble after that and everybody was very pleasant to me in the Sandy Row.

The problem with this type of behaviour is that it makes unionist learners of Irish acceptable to other unionists, but it makes them unacceptable to many Irish-speakers. Thus unionist learners may have to stress their unionism in their own community, but underplay their political beliefs in Irish language circles. Many Protestants feel they have to cultivate an image of studied neutrality to go between both camps. Those that cannot do so, such as relatives of security force members or civil servants, experience great practical difficulties in learning the language.

Working-class learners are troubled by the fact that many of their friends and neighbours perceive Irish to be a republican language. The problems of the Glencairn class are a case in point. The learners struggled with the republican image of the Irish language, particularly since their estate was situated in an interface zone close to Catholic districts of west Belfast. In February 1993, the Glencairn Community Development Association received the following letter:

Dear Sir/Madam

It is with complete disgust that I and many others have read of you running Irish language classes. What next a Glencairn Gaelic team, street names in Irish, a visit from Gerry Adams. There is no chance of the IRA bombing you, as they see fellow travellers. Protestants are being attacked from all directions and their morale is almost nil. The programme on BBC1 concerning Protestants in N. Ireland in general and North Belfast in particular clearly demonstrated this[5]. If you don't realise how this back stabbing scheme will demoralise Protestants even more or how Republicans, Irish speaking Sinn Feiners, the SDLP and others hostile to British Protestants will make splendid propaganda out of it, then you must live under a stone. Protestants who consider themselves to be British and not Irish have their backs against the wall, and we don't need a nest of vipers like you to make things worse. It is bad enough to be attacked by our enemies but for you to do their dirty work for them is sickening. The Glencairn Community Development Association is beginning to be known as the Glencairn Republican Community Development Association. If you have the interests of the Protestant people at heart then we beg you to drop your scheme immediately.

Yours sincerely
Hubert Lister

The learners, all of whom were unionists and very anti-republican in outlook, were outraged by the accusations in the letter, which they dismissed as nonsense. The reference to a 'nest of vipers' seemed to indicate that the writer was, in their words, a harmless 'bible basher'; they would have been far more concerned if they believed the author to have been a member of a loyalist paramilitary grouping. As such, 'Hubert Lister' was not considered to be a danger to the Glencairn group.

However, one learner had personal reasons to reconsider her interest in Irish. Although she was very enthusiastic about the language, she had a crisis of conscience when republican paramilitaries shot her nephew:

> He got shot dead over there at the turn of the road, just over at Ligoneil and at the time it was terrible and all, but then I went to those Irish classes and his mummy says, 'Dot, what are you doing? It's all right for them ones that shot my son, and you're sitting learning their language. It makes you no better than them.' You know, it does make you think.

In learning Irish she appeared to be associating herself with the murderers of her nephew. After an IRA bomb exploded on the Shankill Road on the 25th of October 1993, I telephoned the class organiser, a local community worker, to tell her that I did not wish to take the class in the wake of the explosion. She agreed that it would not be a good idea for the class to continue as feelings were very high in the district.

Later, when I interviewed the community worker, she had decided to abandon learning the language; the republican connotations of the language had become too much for her:

> Well, at the time when I started it I was suiting myself and it was something I wanted to do, but the more I have listened to over the past few months - maybe its because of everything that's went on. The first thing that put me off was the Shankill bomb, you know, and I sat back then and thought you know, 'Why am I doing this? I seem to be going along with these people, people who probably know the Irish language who planted that bomb' And it sort of, I don't know whether that makes sense to anybody, but it was how I felt you know.

Another learner who had attended the class said that she rarely associated Irish with the 'troubles', and the Shankill bomb only temporarily deterred her from learning Irish:

> The only time I saw it connected with the troubles and I felt then it would have been, was just after a major bombing on the Shankill Road, and so many people lost their lives, and the wee guy who planted the bomb, at his funeral, the cameras and the television zoomed up to one of the wreaths and it was written in Irish, and I'm almost sure it was Gerry Adam's wreath, and it was written in

> Irish, and I felt nearly revulsion, you know, because he was carrying the coffin of the wee guy who blew the people up. It, it all sort of tied it too close with the Irish, and just at that time I associated it with the troubles, you know. That was the only time - 'cos he had used the Irish.

Later in the interview she returned to her original interpretation of the language:

> I don't think it should be allowed to be a discriminatory language. It should be for us all. I don't think it should keep the Protestants out. I think we should, its our language as well, you know. It's for Catholics, it's for everybody, its for people from Ireland.

Although her interest in Irish had not been deterred by the Shankill bombing, the class had finished and was not resumed; she would not be able to learn Irish on the estate, whether she wanted to or not.

The experience of the north Down group differed considerably from that of the Glencairn learners. The group had some reservations about going to folk nights in Catholic bars after explosions in Newtownards and Bangor, but none of them were deterred in their efforts to learn Irish. For the north Down learners, the republican image of the language was a mere nuisance, rather than a major psychological obstacle to their learning activities. On the whole, the north Down learners cultivated their interest in their home district and in the Donegal Gaeltacht, circumventing any possible difficulties with the Irish language scene in Belfast[6]. Like many middle-class Protestants, the group removed itself from the ravages of the troubles as much as possible.

Generally speaking, middle-class learners feel that they can tell their friends and relatives that they are learning Irish without fear of serious reprisals. However, for some the language can be a touchy subject that is best avoided in mixed or polite company, as this Cultra learner attests:

> I don't talk a lot about it, because there's no point in raising

hackles unnecessarily. I think many of our community, because it's a social club I belong to, it's a golf club, I simply don't talk about it, about our situation. Maybe because they're afraid of what the future may or may not hold, and we have one of our people on the committee who's lost a son in the RUC and so on. We do have both Protestants and Catholics in our golf club, and everybody's very friendly to everybody else, but we don't talk a lot about the situation openly.

Who is Politicising Irish?

In this section I will explore the attitudes of Protestant learners to the Irish language revival. In discussing the aims of the Irish language movement with the learners, I used a document published in 1993 by the Committee for the Administration of Justice (CAJ), which recommends that the British government support the Irish language revival by implementing a wide range of measures, including state-sponsored bilingualism. The CAJ document uses European and United Nations charters to argue the case for a greater effort by the British government to promote the Irish language in Northern Ireland. The measures proposed include: the right for parents to have their children educated through Irish; the right to use Irish in court and with public bodies; and government support for an all-Ireland television service in Irish. Viewed together, these proposals represent some of the most far-reaching goals of the Irish language movement.

Many Protestant learners of Irish are not well acquainted with the achievements and goals of the Irish language revival; they are particularly unaware of revivalist activities in west Belfast. Their attitudes to the revival are often informed by their own ideological positions:

GMc.: What is the British government's attitude to the Irish language?
Learner: I'm amazed how much they have contributed towards the Irish, and I think that these folk who tell me that they're struggling to set up schools without any government money and,

'How many go to your school?' 'Well, there's six' (laughs).
... *GMc.:* Do you think that people should be allowed to speak Irish in court (CAJ proposal)?'
Learner: If they are genuine Irish speakers and can't speak English, then there should be, but to set up dual-language courts in a country where English is the language seems to be an unnecessary duplication. I don't think you can expect the rest of the community to do this. I don't think we can expect the rest of the community to finance our hobby, which is what it is.
GMc.: What about the proposal that the British and Irish governments should co-operate to provide a cross-border Irish language television channel (CAJ proposal)?
Learner: Well, knowing the Conservative government in England, I don't think there's very much money available. It's amazing the amount of money that's poured into this place. I think the Conservative philosophy is coming to the viewpoint of saying, 'We're not going to put so much money into Northern Ireland' and they will find that the money coming here will be used on much more basic essentials than that. That would seem to be a luxury item. We're not a bilingual community at all.
GMc.: What use is Irish?
Learner: As far as I can understand it's a great cultural pursuit, it's a worthwhile intellectual exercise, it helps us to express our own identity and thought forms and so on. But what use is classical music? I just don't know. I would find it very hard to answer that question.

The speaker draws on the conservative element of Protestant ideology which opposes state interventionism, and he appears to empathise with the policies pursed by the Conservative government. In the first part of the text he echoes unionist disdain at nationalist complaints of deprivation and dependence on government hand-outs (Bruce 1994: 61; Todd 1987: 22). Irish is described as a 'luxury item', a 'cultural pursuit', like classical music. In short, the speaker views Irish as a leisure pursuit that is not within the remit of public funding. This is exactly the representation of the Irish language that the revivalist movement is attempting to refute.

The conception of the Irish language as a leisure pursuit

partly explains Protestant disbelief of the objectives of the Irish language community to create a bilingual community in west Belfast and/or Northern Ireland. Protestant learners live, work and recreate in English language environments in which the Irish language has little immediate relevance. They are not engaged in full-time revivalism to create an Irish language community; most jobs involving the Irish language are located in nationalist districts, areas in which few Protestants would consider working. Protestant learners are more concerned with finding appropriate evening-classes than battling with the Department of Education to secure funding for Irish-medium schools. However, it would be erroneous to suggest that Protestant learners conceive of the Irish language as a mere hobby. Many of them make tremendous efforts and take great risks to learn the language. This indicates that the language is very important to them, even if it does not appear to have a huge impact on their everyday lives.

Protestant learners often oppose some aspects of the revival by the attribution of 'political' motives to those involved in them. In the following texts, the learners express their opinions on the erection of bilingual street-signs:

> I would think, 'What's the ulterior motive to putting it into Irish, when I know that it's in English?' And to me I would not see that as trying to promote the Irish language as such, but you reinforce a certain stance.

> I'm not sure if the people who live on the streets that have Irish street signs speak Irish themselves, or whether it's a 'fuck you' statement to the authorities.

In the first text the speaker claims that those who erect street-signs are not concerned about the welfare of the language, but have an 'ulterior motive'. The second text provides a suggestion as to the nature of this motive; a hostility to the unionist and British authorities. The use of Irish in street-signs is described as a form of boundary-maintenance. Protestant learners often attribute cultural motives to learn Irish to themselves, and 'political' motives for learning and promoting Irish to others, particularly republicans. I asked a member of the north Down group for her opinions on the language revival in Belfast:

> *GMc.:* Do you know anything about the revival in Belfast?
> *Learner:* Not really. We belong to the North Down Gaeltacht (laughs). No, certainly there's a revival in west Belfast, a big interest in Irish-speaking schools. Does Gerry Adams have Irish? Every time he opens his mouth he puts a nail in the coffin of the language for the Prods. I know a guy particularly, who's really interested in Irish, and the other day Gerry Adams said something in Irish and he says, 'That's it.' He finished.
> *GMc.:* Why do you think there's a big interest in Irish in Belfast?
> *Learner:* Political. It's certainly political. It is nothing other than political, they're using the Irish language, they're *abusing* it. Yet nobody minds anyone learning Irish. I think its good that people should know it, but not that way, I don't think it's right. They're entitled to do what they want, of course, but I think its being used politically. It's used in the jails! All the political prisoners in the jails have Irish. They're taking it and making it their own.

The learner places an ideological and geographical barrier between the north Down learners, who learn the Irish language for 'cultural' reasons, and the Irish speakers of west Belfast, who she perceives as manipulating the language for 'political' purposes. She implies that republicans jealously guard Irish from unionists interested in the language. However, her opposition to republicans 'abusing' the Irish language is at variance with her libertarian principles, which permit anyone to learn Irish if they wish.

Protestant learners attribute 'political' motivations to those who do not share their own political outlooks; they accuse others of manipulating the language for cynical reasons and of being uninterested in the language for its own sake. 'Cultural' motives to learn Irish are attributed to themselves to indicate a genuine concern for the welfare of the language and it's future. Learners often attribute positive 'cultural' motives for learning

Irish to themselves, and negative 'political' motives to political opponents. This process often takes the form of constitutional nationalist and unionist learners accusing republicans of 'politicising' the Irish language:

> I think there's a class in Conway Mill (a refurbished mill on the Falls Road) or something, but you're going right into the heart of west Belfast, and I think there's an emphasised political dimension to the learning of it there, which I don't care for. I want to learn the language purely for cultural reasons, not for any other reasons, you know.

Of course, by opposing the involvement of republicans in the Irish language revival, Protestant 'culturists' can be just as 'political' as those they oppose. Indeed, some Protestant nationalists are suspicious about unionists interested in the Irish language, and suspect the latter of having 'political' motives:

> *GMc:* What do you think of Chris McGimpsey learning Irish, and the fact that there are classes on the Shankill?
> *Learner:* I think that everybody should have access to it and have a free choice. The more access there is, the better. But it's like, why? What's the point? If it's not saying something about your identity as an Irish person, I mean if you're learning Irish it's inevitable. I cannot see the point of doing it, other than that. Why would you learn it? Except in a sort of a disruptive way, you know, it's fun to be able to stand up in Belfast City Council to be able to speak more Irish than them, and score a point that way. But I mean for me you want to learn a language because of something positive to say about yourself, and Irish culture, and a sense of place, and there's absolutely no point in being into it to score a point against republicans or nationalists. So maybe I just haven't studied what he's trying to do with it enough, but my impression would be that it's very difficult to do in any kind of positive way.

Here we have the mirror image of the unionist belief that republicans are manipulating the Irish language for political purposes. The speaker describes the connection between the Irish language, culture and nationalism as 'positive'. He suspects unionists of having a negative motive for learning Irish in that he believes they wish to score points over nationalists. However, the speaker is reluctant to oppose unionists learning Irish, as this would conflict with his belief that the language should be available for all who wish to learn it.

The above texts demonstrate that the views of Protestant learners on the language movement are informed by their personal opinions on nationalism and republicanism. However, the imputed connections between nationalism and certain Irish language projects does not result in unionist antipathy to all aspects of the revival. Many are favourable to Irish language programmes on radio and television, as well as Irish-medium education. Protestant learners often express a sense of awe when they meet children who can speak Irish. In the following text, a learner from the Shankill Women's Centre describes a visit to an Irish-medium primary school on the Falls Road:

> It was amazing, absolutely. It was very disciplined, but a very relaxed atmosphere, and the children, right from pre-school, using their Irish to communicate. All their nursery rhymes were in Irish and if they want something they try very hard to make themselves understood ... I mean we went to a P1 class and a P2 class and to a P3 class, and in the P2 class I was lost because I couldn't understand what they were saying! The children all *love* it, and it's a very happy environment.

This learner can identify with the enjoyment the children receive from learning Irish. For her, potentially divisive political issues become unimportant. For many such individuals their common identification as Irish speakers overcomes religious and political issues. In Northern Ireland, interest groups unite people from different backgrounds, but as I have shown, enthusiasts often bring their backgrounds with them.

Conclusion

The differing beliefs and experiences of Protestant learners of Irish are often informed by their class backgrounds. Generally speaking, Protestant working-class learners have more difficulties than middle-class ones. This is because social sanctions are imposed more rigorously in working-class districts than in middle-class ones. Protestant middle-class learners have greater opportunities to bend the rules; some of them even abandon unionism, the main political ideology of Northern Protestants[7].

Middle-class Protestants do not fear community punishment if they reject the values of their peers; thus the north Down group learn Irish, and some of them express a nationalist outlook, without fear of censure from their friends and relatives. Middle-class Protestants often believe themselves to be liberal and non-sectarian; therefore they will not oppose other Protestants who learn Irish. The world-view of middle-class Protestants is facilitated in part by the fact that they often live in peaceful districts, insulated from the violent sectarian strife of working-class areas.

Middle-class learners can diversify their learning experiences on account of their income; they drive to different classes and attend Irish language courses in the Gaeltacht. Their trips to the Republic symbolises the convergence of values of many Southern Irish speakers and Northern Protestant learners; both reject the traditional associations between the Irish language with Catholicism and republicanism.

Because middle-class learners are educated and well-read, they are often able to draw upon realms of knowledge, such as that of a Protestant Gaelic heritage, which are not widely available in the public domain. Such forms of knowledge are used to bypass the Catholic and/or republican image of Irish, and they help Protestant learners to identify with the Irish language.

Middle-class unionists often subscribe to a British/Irish identity; they combine a sense of British citizenship with a regional or cultural sense of Irishness. The north Down group differ from other Protestants in that they are learning Irish, but they attempt to associate the language with the mixed British/

Irish identification of Northern unionists. Some unionist learners believe that by learning Irish they are taking part in an attempt to re-define unionism in terms other than the articulation of an ersatz Englishness.

Some unionists who value the Irish language recommend that unionism should engage nationalism in a contest to define the meaning of the Irish language. They wish to disassociate the language from nationalist ideology and represent it as the property of both religious and political traditions in Ireland. In doing so they tap into two powerful trends in Ireland: the rejection of republicanism, with its perceived monopolisation of aspects of Irish culture; and the adoption of pluralism, which stresses the equal validity and cross-fertilisation of the various cultural traditions on the island.

Protestant working-class learners of Irish have more problems than their middle-class co-religionists. They often fear Catholics and are reluctant to venture into nationalist districts to learn Irish. They are simultaneously envious of and repelled by the culture of their republican 'opponents'. Some of them attempt to appropriate nationalist cultural capital for themselves and for the Ulster national identity of the Protestant working class. This is part of the struggle to define a coherent Protestant cultural identity in Northern Ireland. However, many working-class learners do not have access to the information that would enable them to challenge the dominant republican/Catholic image of the Irish language.

Working-class Protestants who learn Irish often have deep feelings of ambivalence about the language. They are wary of publicising their interest, as many of their neighbours and friends view the Irish language with suspicion. If their interest in Irish becomes well-known, they come under great pressure within their own communities to reject Irish by accepting the relationship between the language and republicanism. On some occasions, learners do so, and abandon learning Irish. Others continue to learn Irish and face punishment if they are unable to demonstrate their loyalty to the Protestant community beyond doubt. Working-class Protestants have little knowledge of how to find Irish classes, and have a restricted choice of learning venues as they often do not have their own means of transport. Given their difficulties, it is not surprising that most of the Protestant learners of Irish whom I encountered were not working-class.

Unionist learners of all classes often perceive the Irish language to be a private activity that should not impinge upon the public British character of the 'province'. They are unnerved by public forms of the Irish language, such as bilingual street signs and the use of Irish language personal names. This is due in part to feelings of ambivalence about certain aspects of the Irish language that are associated with republicans. Middle-class learners cope with this problem by distinguishing the language from its speakers; they represent Irish as part of a 'benign' culture that is manipulated by malevolent political opponents. They create or draw upon images of the language which challenge the views of Irish speakers with whom they disagree. If they feel uncomfortable with certain learning venues, they avoid them and seek alternative ones, some of which are hundreds of miles away. Middle-class learners insulate themselves from republican Irish speakers in the manner in which they escape the full impact of the troubles.

Working-class Protestants, including those who learn Irish, often feel themselves to be in the front line of defence against republicanism, and they resent the Irish language as it is often used in a symbolic fashion by republicans in the media. Working-class learners differ from their middle-class counterparts in that they have more difficulty in disassociating Irish from Catholic/nationalist speakers of the language. Like other members of their class, working-class learners often perceive these Irish speakers to be their adversaries; therefore they experience feelings of ambivalence arising from their desire to learn the 'enemy's' language. Despite their difficulties, some working-class learners display an ability to make the Irish language 'their's' as easily as their middle-class counterparts.

However, the mental mobility of some working-class learners is not matched by a physical one; however enthusiastic they are about the Irish language, the fear of social sanctions from both Catholics and Protestants constrains their ability to tell co-religionists about their interest and find learning venues.

References

Adamson, I, 1974
The Cruithin: The Ancient Kindred. Bangor: Pretani Press.
_____ 1985
The Identity of Ulster. Belfast: Pretani Press.
_____ 1991
The Ulster People. Bangor: Pretani Press.

Breen, R, 1996
'Who Wants a United Ireland? Constitutional Preferences among Catholics and Protestants.' In R. Breen, P. Devine and L. Dowds (eds.) *Social Attitudes in Northern Ireland, 1995-1996.* Belfast: Appletree Press.

Bruce, S, 1994
The Edge of the Union: The Ulster Loyalist Political Vision. Oxford: University Press.

Burton, F, 1978
The Politics of Legitimacy: Struggles in a Belfast Community. London: Routledge and Kegan Paul.

Cohen, A. P. (ed.), 1986
Symbolising Boundaries: Identity and Diversity in British Cultures. Manchester: Manchester University Press.

Committee for the Administration of Justice (CAJ), 1993
Stáid agus Stádas Gaeilge i dTuaisceart na hÉireann/The Irish Language in Northern Ireland: The British Government's Approach to the Irish Language in Light of the European Charter for Regional or Minority Languages. Belfast: CAJ.

Foster, J. W, 1995
'Why I am a Unionist.' In J. W. Foster (ed.) *The Idea of the Union: Statements and Critiques in Support of the Union of Great Britain and Northern Ireland.* Vancouver: Belcouver Press.

McGimpsey, C, 1994
Untitled contribution to P. Mistéil (ed.) *The Irish Language and the Unionist Tradition.* Belfast: Ulster People's College/ULTACH Trust.

Moxon-Browne, E, 1991
'National Identity in Northern Ireland.' In P. Stringer and G. Robinson (eds.) *Social Attitudes in Northern Ireland, 1990-1.* Belfast: Blackstaff Press.

Tannen, D, 1989
Talking Voices: Repetition, Dialogue and Imagery in Conversational Discourse. Cambridge: Cambridge University Press.

Todd, J, 1987
'Two Traditions in Unionist Political Culture.' *Irish Political Studies* **2**: 1-26.

_____ 1994
'Irish Pluralism in a European Perspective'. *Études Irlandaises* **XIX**-1: 155-165.

Tovey, H, Hannan, D, and Abramson, H, 1989.
Why Irish? Irish Identity and the Irish Language. Dublin: Bord na Gaeilge.

Waddell, N, and Cairns, E, 1986
'Situational Perspectives on Social Identity in Northern Ireland.' *British Journal of Social Psychology* **25**: 25-31.

Footnotes

1. Chris McGimpsey is a Ulster Unionist Party councillor and Irish language enthusiast. His views on the Irish language have been published in *'The Irish Language and the Unionist Tradition'* (1994).

2. Of the remaining 23% of learners, some declined to offer a definite opinion on the border, or I judged from the nervousness of the respondents that it would be unwise to discuss political issues with them.

3. The song was *'Óró, Sé do Bheatha 'bhaile'.*

4. Adamson's interpretation of the Irish language has been published in a series of works (Adamson 1974, 1985, 1991).

5. The programme in question was a BBC Northern Ireland

'Spotlight' production relating to demographic changes threatening the survival of Protestant communities in north Belfast and Fermanagh.

6. Two of the learners eventually went to Irish classes in Belfast, including west Belfast, as there were no more suitable classes in their home district.

7. None of the working-class learners I met were nationalist in outlook.

Aspects of the Irish language movement:
AODÁN MAC PÓILIN

The language movement must be seen initially as a reaction to the disastrous decline of Irish as a spoken tongue in the nineteenth century. The scale of decline can be illustrated through the Census returns of the period. For example, the 1891 Census shows that while 100% of over 60s in the Barony of Kinnataloon in Co Cork were Irish-speakers, no children under ten could speak the language (Nic Craith 1993, 111). On a national scale, Garrett Fitzgerald has shown from an analysis of the 1881 Census that at least 45% of those born in Ireland in the first decade of the 19th century were Irish-speakers (Fitzgerald 1984, 127). Figures from the 1891 Census, while they record 680,174 speakers of Irish in Ireland (14.5% of the population), most of whom can be assumed to be native speakers, they also show that only 3.5% of those born in the 1880s were brought up speaking the language (Hindley 1990, 15, 19).

The first effective mass movement to counteract this trend came with the founding of the Gaelic League in 1893. The original aim of the League was the maintenance of the language in the Gaeltacht, the areas in which Irish had survived as a spoken language. However, although the League may have helped slow the decline of the language in historic Irish-speaking areas, this decline was neither halted nor reversed. Paradoxically, the main ideological impact of the language movement was not in the Gaeltacht, but among English-speaking nationalists.

In effect, the League developed both a conservationist and a revivalist role in pre-partition Ireland, both roles being subsequently adopted by the southern state. It is, I believe, important to distinguish between these aspects of the language movement. Language conservation involves maintaining a language as a vernacular within communities which already use it. Revival involves restoring a language as a vernacular to areas and communities to which it has been lost: in the case of Irish, this involved some communities which had not spoken the language for hundreds of years. Because the conditions for maintenance and revival are significantly different, and because the distinction between the two processes has been constantly underemphasised, I would like at this point to examine the dynamic underpinning each of them separately.

Language maintenance

The continuity of all linguistic groups depends on what I will call here linguistic momentum. By this I mean the forces which ensure that a language is used in society and passed on from one generation to the next. In the case of dominant and expanding language groups, the engine which drives the momentum of language use is the control of society by that group, the high status which such control confers, and the necessity of using the language to function in society.

A different kind of momentum applies to the continuity of minority language groups. Most minority languages have survived through their being rooted in traditional linguistic communities. Even then, their survival as community languages can depend on a complex of internal and external factors, including geographic and social isolation, ethnic identity, ideology, or high status within a significant social institution, even, in fact, lack of opportunity to learn the dominant language. Without such supportive socio-linguistic conditions, you have a kind of residual linguistic momentum, which resembles nothing more than a car whose engine has been turned off. The car may still be moving, but the impetus which sustained its momentum has been lost, and it will inevitably grind to a halt.

Ireland in the latter half of the 19th century illustrates not only how fast a language can decline, but also how it *can* survive in the face of overwhelmingly hostile social and political forces, without a support structure, and in spite of the apparent complicity of the communities themselves in its loss. In those scattered - and usually remote - areas where Irish did survive, a significant proportion of the community were monoglot Irish-speakers, near-monoglots, people who were more comfortable or expressive speaking Irish than English, or who had built up relationships with other members of the community through Irish. In these conditions, Irish was the language which was spoken naturally and instinctively in important language domains, even where most of the speakers may have been functionally bilingual.

The conservationist policy of the post-independence southern state was based on the state's ideological commitment to the preservation of the language. Its purpose was to maintain the historic Gaeltacht, and ultimately to facilitate its expansion.

However, the dynamic of language shift from Irish to English was already well established. In spite of the new supportive ideology and the high formal status of Irish within the state - which was often more formal than actual - many Gaeltacht communities continued to be affected by sociolinguistic forces militating against Irish, as well as the demoralisation which had destroyed Irish as a community language in the rest of the country, and the residual contempt of Anglophone communities for their Irish-speaking neighbours. Instead of an expanding Gaeltacht, Irish-speaking communities continued to switch from Irish to English - although more slowly than before - even after independence, a pattern of language shift which has not been reversed. It had been hoped that Irish would be restored as a community language in areas which were already shifting towards English, and in which the younger generation had lost the language. This expectation appears to have been completely confounded. Except for a small transplanted community of native speakers in Co Meath, Irish as a significant community language today exists only in areas in which the younger generation were brought up with Irish as their first language three generations ago. Nor have all such areas survived as Gaeltachts. Estimates of the number of habitual Irish-speakers living in the widely scattered Gaeltacht areas vary considerably, but are still very small. In 1981, Desmond Fennell estimated it as being less than 30,000 (Fennell 1981, 35-36). In 1990, Reg Hindley - a much more hostile observer - calculated it at a maximum of 10,000 (Hindley 1990, 251).

The historic Gaeltacht is facing a crisis, and its long-term future is now in question. Most younger Gaeltacht people can express themselves as well in Irish as in English, which is dominating an increasing number of language domains within Gaeltacht communities. The smaller size of these scattered communities, greater social contact with monolingual English-speakers, and the repatriation of English-speaking children of emigrants, have also affected the sociolinguistic dynamics within the historic Gaeltacht. Many native speakers are choosing English as their normal means of communication, and fewer Gaeltacht families are bringing up their children as Irish-speakers. Irish as a language of communication within Gaeltacht communities is becoming increasingly a matter of conscious choice rather than instinct.

Language Revival in Southern Ireland

Where language maintenance aims to support an historic linguistic status quo, language revival is primarily aimed at reversing the linguistic status quo, and creating a bilingual society from a monolingual one.

The first step in reviving a language is essentially propagandistic. It involves persuading as many people as possible of the value of the language and engaging their support. Because positive attitudes to Irish are meaningless without a pool of speakers of the language, the second stage involves language acquisition. The language movement in Ireland has always expended a great deal of its energy on consciousness raising campaigns and language-teaching, and has had a remarkable level of success in these two stages.

A dramatic change in attitude to the language, restricted largely to nationalists, from its lowest point in the late nineteenth century to a high level of esteem has been achieved. In the southern state this esteem probably peaked in the twenties and thirties of the twentieth century, partly because Irish figured centrally in the process of political and social consolidation of the post-independence decades, and partly because it was widely believed that the revival process would be successful. The intensive process of gaelicisation which was instigated during the 1920s was mainly focused on the civil service and the education system. Its triumph was in creating a significant pool of largely middle-class speakers of Irish as a second language. The latest Census indicates that about a million people in the Republic of Ireland have learned enough Irish to record themselves as Irish-speakers. Many of these learners have a strong emotional and ideological commitment to the language, and this group includes most of the prominent figures in the language movement, and a number of influential leaders of opinion and decision-makers.

This achievement should not be dismissed: the Republic of Ireland is possibly the only country in the world where learners of a language outnumber native speakers (most speakers of Hebrew in Israel are now native speakers). The gaelicisation process in the south did, however, fail to reverse the decline of the Gaeltacht, and failed to create new language communities. It also, ultimately, led to a backlash against Irish from those who felt that the education system failed them, from those whose commitment to the language had never been wholehearted, from almost all unionists, and from a large number of nationalists for whom the language had a subsidiary role or was irrelevant.

This last group had been largely silent in the pre-independence period, partly because of the imperative to maintain a show of unity, and partly because the language issue was an extremely useful part of the nationalist armoury. While the country was ruled from London, the Irish language movement could be looked on as both a symbol of nationhood and as a tool for opposing British rule. While desirable, it was not absolutely necessary to go to the trouble of learning or using the language to utilise it either as a symbol or as a means of resistance. This is clear from the advice given by Henry Morris in 1903 during the campaign to have mail addressed in Irish accepted - and delivered - by the Post Office, which at its height saw 600 items addressed in Irish being submitted *daily*. (Details of the campaign were filed in the London Post Office in bulky folders labelled 'Correspondence addressed in Erse'):

> Those ... who can write the whole letter in Irish should do so, but those who cannot do that much should at least address the letter in Irish - and in Irish only - except in cases where great dispatch is necessary (Dunleavy 1991, 234).

This nationalist, anti-British, oppositionalist motive lost much of both its function and its force in post-independence southern Ireland, ironically, just at the period when an intense government-inspired drive to revive Irish was in progress. Nationalists whose support for Irish had been inspired mainly by political considerations, while they may have continued to pay lip-service to the ideals of the revival, were inevitably less fervent after independence, particularly when the difficulties facing the revival could no longer be blamed on the British. There developed, in fact, a considerable degree of ambivalence to the revival of Irish. This ambivalence may explain why some of the revivalist policies were so unrealistic, and why many of those which were realistic were carried out so ineffectively. The late Colmán Ó Huallacháin, in two important books reconstructed from his notes, has written scathingly on what he calls the emblematic use of Irish in the southern state:

> Certain things done about Irish owe their importance to their use as a particular kind of outward sign, while the degree to which those involved are affected may be minimal from the point of view of actual understanding or use of the language for

communication. ... Of course ... the use of language may be seen as a symbol... However, the kind of relationship between the symbol and what it symbolises can vary. In the case of Irish, it is helpful, for clarification of important aspects of its development in society during this century, to characterise as 'emblematic' its employment as a symbol having only minimal, if any, reference to communication in society though, at the same time, conveying some kind of reference to ethnic distinctiveness (Ó Huallacháin 1994, 58).

It is worth noting also at this stage both that emblematic use of language may frequently feature in political manoeuvring, and that, in educational matters, such use can lead to ambivalence. The inclusion and fostering of a language as a subject on the curriculum might well be sufficient to satisfy people emblematically, without involving the measures which would be necessary if there were to be tangible results with reference to acquisition of communicative ability in, and use of, the language in society (Ó Huallacháin 1991, 107).

The weakness of the language revival in both parts of Ireland relates to 'use of the language in society'. The majority of people who can speak Irish do not in fact use it regularly in their daily lives. Whether or not this large number of people who know the language but do not use it can be described as a 'language community' may be to stretch the term 'community' beyond its normal use. Because the term 'language community' can be so imprecise, this paper adopts the term 'active language community' to describe those in anglicised areas of Ireland who, through an act of will or choice, use the language frequently in their daily lives.

At this point, I would like to introduce an argument which may appear to be breathtakingly obvious, but does not always receive the attention it deserves. This involves recognition of the fact that some groups of speakers of a language have more linguistic significance than others, and that this significance is related less to the number of speakers than to the degree to which the language is integrated into the daily life of its users, their social coherence, and - most importantly if the language is to survive - the community's ability to successfully regenerate itself as a speech community.

Obviously, active speakers of Irish are more linguistically significant than those who know the language but rarely or never use it. Even then, I would argue that the revivalist active language communities are less significant than the organic language communities of the historic Gaeltacht. Even small demoralised Gaeltacht communities have greater potential for long-term survival than anything the revival has produced after more than a hundred years of effort.

The language movement has failed to create new language communities in which the language is integrated in a meaningful way into the lives of its speakers, and in which the community has meaningful social cohesion. Its most challenging task, besides the maintenance of the language within the historic Gaeltacht, is to create new significant linguistic communities.

How that can be done is the central problem facing the language revival. One important contribution to this debate has been made by Joshua Fishman, who, in his influential book *Reversing Language Shift*, has developed a systematic - if rather mechanistic - approach to language maintenance and revival.

Fishman devotes an entire chapter of his book to an analysis of the language revival in the Republic of Ireland. According to this analysis, the strategy adopted in the Republic has resulted in what he describes as a remarkably stable level of language maintenance. This maintenance, however, involves the transmission of the language through several generations as a second language. Learners of the Irish as a second language teach Irish to a new generation of English-speakers which in its turn teaches it - as a second language - to yet another generation of English-speakers. The weakness Fishman perceives in this strategy is that every generation must meet and overcome the same challenges: rather than surpass the achievements of the previous generation, each new generation must struggle to keep up with the one that went before.

Ultimately, Fishman makes the case that long-term language survival depends on the language domain of the most basic social unit, the family. He argues that the most essential element in the survival and growth of a minority language involves what he calls inter-generational transmission - the passing on of the language from parents to children, supplemented by the building of social contacts between such families. Fishman does acknowledge the value of teaching threatened languages, and activities aimed at increasing the status, recognition and support structures of the language in society. However, he argues strongly that, unless the stage of intergenerational transmission is attained, all other revival policies are unlikely to succeed: 'success in intergenerationally unimportant functions is merely camouflaged failure'; 'the road to societal [language] death is paved with language activity that is not focused on intergenerational continuity' (Fishman 1991, 86, 91).

In Ireland, the number of scattered Irish-speaking families which have developed a self-sustaining social network over a number of generations is comparatively small, and there has been a critical failure to create new organic speech communities. This may have been the most significant failure of the language movement in both parts of Ireland. We have failed, almost entirely, to create new self-sustaining Irish-speaking communities. In spite of significant investment in the language of time, energy, and, in the Republic, money, except for one tiny community in Northern Ireland, not a single city, town, village, townland or street of Irish-speakers has been developed among anglicised communities.

Paradoxically, the failure to create new significant language communities can be partly explained through the concept of linguistic momentum. That linguistic momentum which allowed Irish to survive against enormous pressures in pockets of the country is now working in favour of English, and is, in spite of the best efforts of the revivalists, effectively inhibiting the development of Irish as a community language outside the

Gaeltacht.

One of the problems of the revival is that we have either failed to recognise, or have consistently underestimated, just how difficult it is to create new viable language communities in the context of a largely monoglot society which speaks one of the world's dominant tongues. The revival's over-dependence on promoting Irish in the education system was based on the assumption that use would follow knowledge. We have found, to our cost, that it does not necessarily do so, and our understanding of the sociolinguistic dynamics involved are still underdeveloped. At this point, I would like to try to identify some of the problems involved in creating new language communities.

I would argue that a sustainable new minority language community in which the language is transferred from generation to generation, although it may be originally inspired by ideology, ultimately needs to be underpinned by an internal social dynamic which can transcend the initial impulse. To draw a possibly dubious analogy, the motive for marrying is rarely the same motive which keeps you married.

The creation of such a community will depend in the first instance on Irish-speakers who have made a conscious commitment to the language. Its maintenance over a number of generations will depend on the creation of an environment in which its members find themselves speaking the language automatically and instinctively rather than as a conscious, willed act of defiance against the forces of society. If this argument is sustainable, the creation of social domains in which the language is dominant, but in which the language movement is not itself the focus, is the most important element in the creation of new organic language communities. It is, however, remarkably difficult to create a new social environment in which speaking Irish is felt to be the natural thing to do.

The dynamics which underpinned the historic Gaeltacht cannot be reproduced: monoglot Irish-speaking grandparents cannot be conjured out of the air. Nor can the language be saved by trying to reverse the brutal social forces of the past which brought Irish to the brink of extinction. The experience of several hundred years of living next door to, and under the control of one of the most powerful nations in the world, military defeat, social marginalisation, legal sanctions, mass emigration and ultimately famine cannot (and should not) be imitated. Only a few language enthusiasts, possibly driven by desperation, advocate the disuse of English: most espouse bilingualism. In any social situation, there will therefore always be a choice of languages for those who are bilingual, and none for monoglot speakers of the majority language. The implications of the imbalance of socio-linguistic pressures in favour of English, and against Irish, are therefore considerable.

Another problem involves the difficulties many learners of Irish face in changing their normal language of communication from a language they have spoken since infancy and which everyone in their society can speak, a language of major status which is the dominant language of the mass media, to a second language with an unstable social base. Many learners of Irish also find to their dismay that they do not have the same linguistic resources or range in the second language, and speak English more fluently and more richly. Even children from Irish-speaking homes can find that they are more expressive in English than in Irish in some linguistic domains by the time they reach their teens.

This combination of social and linguistic pressures leads many who have attempted to become involved at some stage of their lives in creating a new language community to effectively abandon the language. The country, in fact, is littered with failed *Gaeilgeoirí*, some of them disillusioned and filled with resentment and a sense of failure or self-contempt, others adopting a range of strategies, from denial to feigned indifference. At their worst, former enthusiasts can involve themselves in the worst kinds of tokenism and jobbery. The sense of desperation felt by those who remain committed to the language can sometimes result in an impossibilist, theatrical fanaticism.

Irish in Northern Ireland

At present the revivalist movement, north and south, is based almost entirely on ideological commitment, and there are both close similarities and marked differences between the revivalist situation in the two parts of the country.

The most significant difference is that the post-independence revival in southern Ireland has received massive support: it has, in fact, been largely state-sponsored and state-led. The revival of Irish has, or had, an important place within the official state orthodoxy. Irish is enshrined in the Constitution as the first of the state's two official languages, and the state officially sponsors a bilingual Ireland as one of its aims. The government of the Republic has invested significantly, although not always effectively, in a wide variety of initiatives to promote Irish through, for example, the educational system, the arts and broadcasting.

The position of Irish is in some ways more complex in the Republic than in Northern Ireland. Because the state pursues both a revivalist and a conservationist programme, there can be unresolved tensions on a policy level between the needs of the minority Gaeltacht communities and the perceived needs of the far larger - and far more influential - minority of non-Gaeltacht Irish-speakers. The entire issue is further complicated by the implications of the official status of Irish within the state, earlier unrealistic expectations of the progress of the revival, an element of ambivalence towards the language issue, and the progressive disengagement of the state from the ideals of the revival. It appears clear that, particularly since the 1960s, although the formal status of the language remains unchanged, the state appears to have been engaged in an elaborate deathbed ritual: the intensity of its protestations of support for the language in inverse proportion to its commitment. Although state support for the language has become increasingly tokenistic, and in spite of the growing recognition that many of the state's earlier policies have failed, many language activists believe, probably correctly, that any diminution of the formal status of Irish is a prelude to its complete marginalisation within Irish society. As a result, a great deal of energy is wasted in the demoralising process of fighting to protect the language's present - in Ó Huallacháin's term - emblematic status.

These complexities do not affect the revival movement in the north, which has to deal with a quite different set of problems. When Northern Ireland was established as a distinct political entity in the 1920s, organic Irish-speaking communities within the new state had almost disappeared. A scattering of older native speakers in residual Gaeltachts in four of the six counties of Northern Ireland had died by the middle of the century. However, new generations of revivalist Irish-speakers continued to emerge. The central defining reality of the Irish language movement in Northern Ireland is that it is essentially and unambiguously a revivalist phenomenon. As the state is at worst hostile and at best indifferent, there is no formal constitutional status to defend, and language activists do not face the frustrations of dealing with official ambivalence, double-speak or double-think.

Because it is clearly understood that the dominant social and political forces in society are inimical to the language, language activists in Northern Ireland focus on the revival within the context of an anglicised society. Irish-speakers exist and are sustained entirely by the ideology of the language movement and the largely voluntary efforts of the revivalists.

The Northern Ireland Census of 1991, the first since 1911 to include a question on knowledge of Irish, recorded 142,003 positive responses (Census 1992, 159). The Census returns also indicated that knowledge of Irish is largely confined to Catholics. A surprisingly large number (over 5,500), given that Irish is rarely taught in non-Catholic schools, identified themselves as belonging to other denominations, and the religion of almost 10,000 was not stated (Census 1993, 28). Unfortunately, as the Census question did not allow for an assessment of levels of fluency, it is difficult to identify the exact number of fluent speakers of the language. In any case, the exact number of fluent Irish-speakers is less important than the fact that they exist at all.

Irish in Northern Ireland faced enormous hostility from the state until very recently. Only one party, the Ulster Unionist Party, held power from the early twenties until 1972. Unionist ideology under the new state involved a conscious rejection of any identification with Ireland beyond the geographical, and the embracing of an ersatz 'British' cultural identity. On 15th August 1945, when the nationalist MP Eddie McAteer used a few words of Irish in Parliament, he was interrupted by the Prime Minister, Sir Basil Brooke, and the Minister of Education, Lieutenant-Colonel Hall-Thompson, with calls of: 'No foreign language here', and forbidden to continue speaking in Irish (Andrews 1997). Although Scottish Gaelic and Welsh programmes had been broadcast by the BBC since the 1920s, Irish was banned from BBC Northern Ireland for fifty years (Andrews 1992, 25 - 37). The language still has no official status in Northern Ireland.

The survival of Irish in Northern Ireland was a considerable achievement, and reflects the enormous dedication of those involved in the movement. In one important development, a group of parents who had learned Irish as a second language built a small estate, *Pobal Feirste*, in Belfast. This now contains seventeen houses, and, small as it is, is the largest concentration of Irish-speaking families in Ireland outside the Gaeltacht. Belfast also has an Irish-language social club, and a cultural centre which houses an Irish-language newspaper, a bookshop, a cafe, a publishing house, an arts centre, a theatre and several groups which are developing the economic potential of the language. Other parts of Northern Ireland reflect similar vitality. A recent development - as recent as the 1970s - is the phenomenon of Irish-medium education, now focused largely on children from English-speaking homes. At the moment more than a thousand children in Northern Ireland attend Irish-medium schools, some of which do not receive government funding. It may be useful to note that there is a (completely misplaced) perception in Ireland that the language is actually more secure in Northern Ireland than in the Republic.

The relationship between the language movement and Irish nationalism has been explored in another essay in this book. There are now some significant differences between the relationship between nationalism and the language movement in the two parts of Ireland. As has been noted, involvement in and support for the language movement in pre-independence Ireland was often based on an impulse to resist the forces of the British state. With independence, this motive disappeared in southern Ireland, where it was discovered that what is acceptable, indeed liberating, as an oppositional, anti-establishment ideology is often seen as oppressive when it becomes established as the official orthodoxy. In the south the promotion of Irish as a focus of nationalist resistance is now largely seen as irrelevant, except among those who ascribe to theories of post-colonialism, and those who hark back with nostalgia to the simplicities of the pre-independence oppositionalist movement and envy the apparent simplicities of the movement in the north of Ireland.

For this and a complex of other reasons, including the decline of the unitary nation-state within the European Union, and a current re-examination of the history and ideology of the state within Irish society, the ideology of the language movement, particularly in the Republic, is now undergoing a process of re-definition. The early revivalist ideology had been based largely, though not exclusively, on a form of nationalism which identified the language as the indispensable, defining essence of the nation, and a particularly reductive essentialism became the basis of the revival during the first decades of the southern state.

This formulation is now generally avoided, partly as a result of the conflict in the north, partly because it has been associated with what is now seen as an unattractive life-denying official orthodoxy, partly because the state has so obviously failed in its attempt to revive Irish as a national language, partly due to resentment that the language has sometimes been used for short-term political ends, partly in reaction to the mindset which concentrated on emblematic issues rather than the building of speech communities, and partly because of increasing awareness of other minority language models. This is accompanied by a growing disappointment that the nationalist impetus which gave the earlier language movement its focus has been insufficient to create new self-sustaining speech communities, north or south.

The cluster of new formulations now emerging around the language issue tend to avoid essentialist definitions deriving ultimately from nationalist ideology, but rather concentrate on a kind of non-dogmatic cultural ecology - cultural continuity, cultural pluralism, the validity and value of minority identities, Irish as a source of personal enrichment. While this shift in the revivalist ideology may sometimes be a rationalisation of a nationalism which dares not speak its name, it also reflects an approach which is shared by some other minority language groups in other parts of the world.

The Northern Ireland language revival exists in a kind of ideological time-warp, as the context of the language movement is in some ways closer to that of pre-partition Ireland than to the present movement in the south. Both inside and outside the language movement in Northern Ireland, there is often an association, or perceived association, between the language movement and resistance to the state, and, for many people, their initial engagement with the language was sparked by an oppositional impulse. There is no doubt that political nationalism often provides the stimulus for involvement in the language movement in Northern Ireland, and is, in fact, the source of much of the vitality of the present phase of the movement here.

Northern Ireland, however, has its own set of internal complexities. Nationalists are in a minority in the state, and there are other tensions and sources of conflict both within society and within the language movement which are not reflected in the south - between Catholic and Protestant, nationalist and unionist, constitutional and non-constitutional nationalist. As can be imagined, in the highly politicised atmosphere in Northern Ireland, any association of the language movement with nationalism can produce an equal and opposite response to the language from the unionist community. Although unionists are alienated by revivalist arguments based on Irish nationalism, the dominant discourse within Northern Ireland, a perspective on the Irish language related to that now developing in southern Ireland can prove attractive to them. It is, however, likely that, unless they can be convinced that space is being made for a unionist perspective within the language movement in Northern Ireland, unionist involvement will be minimal.

There are three sets of impetus which may help create that space. Some language enthusiasts - often nationalists themselves - are deeply concerned at the alienation of unionists from the language, and are prepared to take measures to create the space within the movement for a unionist perspective. Others share the new perspectives developing in southern Ireland based on principles which transcend nationalist ideology. A third element involves increasing exposure to and co-operation with language movements in other societies. In particular, there has been a marked increase in the level of interest in and degree of contact between the Irish language community in Northern Ireland and Gaelic-speaking Scotland. Professor Donald MacLeod, in an article in the *West Highland Free Press* has called attention to the fact that the Scottish Gaeltacht involves both: '... a Celtic Protestantism and a British Catholicism' (MacLeod 1994, 9). Whether or not these developments will translate into significant unionist involvement in the language is impossible to predict. However, within a language movement which, in the past, drew its main strength from nationalist political ideology, there is a significant and growing resistance to being labelled or confined by political formulations, and a new openness and generosity of spirit which may make unionist involvement a reality.

References

Andrews 1992
Liam Andrews, 'BBC Northern Ireland and the Irish Language: the Background'. In Mac Póilin, A, and Andrews, L, *BBC agus an Ghaeilge / BBC and the Irish Language*, Belfast, Iontaobhas ULTACH / ULTACH Trust, 25-37.

Andrews 1997
Liam Andrews, Untitled thesis in progress on the history of the Irish language in Northern Ireland, Queens University, Belfast. The references quoted are from *Official Report of Debates, Parliament of Northern Ireland*, 1945 - 46, XXIX, Belfast, HMSO, Cols. 369 & 533 - 534.

Census 1992
The Northern Ireland Census 1991, Summary Report, Belfast, Her Majesty's Stationary Office.

Census 1993
Northern Ireland Census 1991, Irish Language Report, Belfast HMSO.

Dunleavy 1991
Janet Egleson Dunleavy, & Gareth W Dunleavy, *Douglas Hyde, a Maker of Modern Ireland*, Berkeley, University of California Press.

Fennel 1981
Desmond Fennel, 'Can a Shrinking Linguistic Minority be saved?' In E Haughen, J D McClure, D S Thomson (eds), *Minority Languages Today*. Edinburgh, Edinburgh University Press.

Fishman 1991
Joshua Fishman, *Reversing Language Shift*, Cleveland, Multilingual Matters.

Fitzgerald 1984
Fitzgerald, Garret, 'Estimates for baronies on minimum level of Irish among successive decennial cohorts: 1771-1781 to 1861-1871', *Proceedings of the Royal Irish Academy*, 84c, 117-155.

Hansard 1992
House of Commons Parliamentary Debates (Hansard), Vol 214, Written Answers, London, HMSO, 1993, 17 November, 1992, Cols.149 - 152.

Hindley 1990
Reg Hindley, *The Death of the Irish Language, a qualified obituary*, London & New York, Routledge.

MacLeod 1994
Donald MacLeod, 'Footnotes', *West Highland Free Press*, 16th September 1994, 9.

Nic Craith 1993
Máiréad Nic Craith, *Malartú Teanga: An Ghaeilge i gCorcaigh sa Naoú hAois Déag*, Bremen, Cumann Eorpach Léann na hÉireann.

Ó Huallacháin 1991
Colmán Ó Huallacháin, *The Irish Language in Society*, Mícheál Ó Murchú (Ed), Coleraine, University of Ulster.

Ó Huallacháin 1994
Colmán Ó Huallacháin, *The Irish and Irish - a sociolinguistic analysis of the relationship between a people and their language*, Rónán Ó Huallacháin, Patrick Conlan (Eds), Dublin, Irish Franciscan Provincial Office.

Ó Riain 1994
Seán Ó Riain, *Pleanáil Teanga in Éirinn, 1919 - 1985*, Dublin, Carbad/Bord na Gaeilge.

Can linguistic minorities cope with a favourable majority?
ANTAINE Ó DONNAILE

Introduction

This, I am sure, seems to be a strange question. One's immediate assumption is that a linguistic minority might cope very well with the support of a majority community. Some might argue that they should count themselves very lucky when they get it. In this essay I examine some of the processes involved in minority-majority relations and look at their implications with particular reference to their effect on the Irish-speaking community in Northern Ireland.

It could be argued that speakers of Irish are currently in an enviable position on both sides of the border. The southern state has always given the language a high status, and, since 1938, it has been the first official language of the state. In 1996, a mainly English-speaking government funded the establishment of *Teilifís na Gaeilge*, a development which has given the language a significant boost. It is clear that Irish speakers do not form the majority of the population in the Republic of Ireland, yet despite the protests of some very vocal commentators, the population in general is very favourable to its Irish-speaking minority. Surveys initiated by the Linguistics Institute of Ireland twenty years ago have demonstrated a consistent pattern: although only approximately 25% of the population claimed reasonable ability in the language, most of the remaining 75% were supportive of it, and only 20% were against its promotion (CILAR 1975:28, 1985).

In Northern Ireland it can without doubt be argued that there is, and has been, a significant level of hostility to the Irish language both at official level and in the community. In spite of this Irish speakers have begun to receive levels of support which would have been unthinkable ten years ago. Irish speakers form almost 10% of the northern population (according to generous self-assessment in the 1991 census), and the language now receives a level of government recognition, as illustrated in the following recent statement from a senior civil servant:

> The government recognises that the Irish language is perceived by many people in Northern Ireland as an important part of their cultural heritage. It respects the special importance of Irish, encourages interest in it and appreciation of it, and highlights its contribution to the cultural heritage of the whole community.
> What this means in practical terms is that Government will respond positively, where practicable, to soundly based requests for assistance. In the last financial year, the Government spent £2m on projects with an Irish language dimension. The second practical manifestation is the removal of unnecessary obstacles to the wider use of the language, e.g. the recent repeal of the 1949 legislation on street names. (Tony Canavan from CCRU 1995 - Speaking in *Cultúrlann Mac Adam - Ó Fiaich* at a conference organised by *Comhdháil Náisiúnta na Gaeilge*.)

Other manifestations of majority support for the minority include an increasing number of grants for Irish-medium education: two schools to receive grant-aid recently are a primary school in Newry, *Bunscoil an Iúir,* and *Meánscoil Feirste,* the first fully funded Irish language secondary school in Northern Ireland. Added to this is the work of government-sponsored bodies such as the ULTACH Trust, The Arts Council of Northern Ireland, Making Belfast Work and BBC Northern Ireland's Irish language service. The language is also supported by many thousands of English-speaking private individuals and a number of organisations. *Forbairt Feirste* in West Belfast, a recently-founded development agency which receives significant grant-aid from various bodies, appears to be very successful in the promotion of employment through the Irish language. Irish as a medium for entertainment and for communication is becoming more and more commonplace. In 1996 we witnessed one of the first Irish language plays in the Lyric Theatre Belfast and another is planned this year. The recently opened Waterfront Hall in Belfast has hosted several nights featuring Irish music and language. In this environment one could argue that the Irish speaking community in the North is coping very well with the goodwill it now receives and with the money and support at various levels.

It can and should be stated that this present level of support in the North is the result of years of struggle and hardship on the part of Irish speakers and that most Irish speakers are less than happy with current provision for the language. To question the minority group's ability to cope with this support and tolerance, however, may indeed seem strange. That however is exactly what I'm going to do. This article doesn't intend to provide any black and white answers (which rarely exist, especially when dealing with minority or threatened cultures). I hope, rather, to encourage questioning and debate and perhaps to promote new ways of looking at old issues. It is through openness and continuous questioning that we re-evaluate stale interpretations of social processes and it is through civilized discussion that we give languages and their speakers the respect they deserve.

Language is, without doubt, an issue which deserves respect. Language for everyone who has an ability to communicate in any way is one of the most important, most sophisticated and also most humanising gifts we have. In the process of learning a language, whatever language that is, we learn how to interpret and map the world, how that world views us and ours. We learn how to speak and behave appropriately among our own and other groups. We learn about ourselves as individuals and as community or family. Therefore to criticise the linguistic behaviour of others, to indicate that they do not speak properly or to belittle their dialect or language, can cause hurt or even anger at personal, public or even political levels. Similarly, people can feel threatened by hearing a language or dialect with which they are not familiar or do not understand or which does not correspond with their own standards. Analysis of these phenomena can add not only to our understanding of the importance of linguistic issues today, but relate them to the political and religious complexities of our own society.

The key phrases in my discussion are commonly used in modern day sociolinguistics or the sociology of language. They are 'language and power' and 'language and social network' (e.g. Milroy 1982, Ó Riagáin 1993, Ó Donnaile 1994). The 'language and power' concept views a particular language or dialect as a form of 'cultural capital,' an accessory which can enrich or impoverish the position of the user in a certain society depending on the value placed on it by that society. The other concept of 'language and social network' is strongly related to the first and links language maintenance, change or shift to the maintenance, changing or shifting which occurs within social networks or communities - whatever their size. The basic thesis of 'language and social network' is that strong close-knit communities act as linguistic fortresses contributing significantly to language or dialect maintenance by defending their members from cultural pressures in the society at large. This article examines the position of Irish-speakers in relation to both approaches before making some suggestions about the implications for them of official support from the larger language group.

Language and Power

Before I discuss whether minorities can cope with a favourable majority I would like to consider if minorities can cope with any majority. It is reckoned by Krauss (1992:7) that there are about 6,000 human languages spoken in the world at present - 81% of these languages are in Asia and in Africa. Krauss believes that 40% of them are now effectively moribund. It is believed that at the present rate of language shift, the coming century will see 90% - 5,400 of the world's languages - either lost or in their final stages of decline. Academics agree that all these endangered languages have one thing in common: they are all in contact with larger, or more powerful, linguistic groups. The very state of belonging to a linguistic minority in close contact with a larger group is therefore dangerous.

When one looks at the societal power wielded by a powerful language it is clear that its strength does not derive from certain intrinsic virtues or strengths. It is the power which is wielded or which is perceived to be wielded by its speakers which ensures that the language becomes powerful. Similarly, when other groups may be perceived as, for example, weak, vulgar, poetic, romantic etc., their languages are often thought to have the same attributes. It should be noted that, although these groups are described here as minorities, reflecting current realities, marginalised and disempowered groups can sometimes represent the numerical majority of their society.

Power relationships even influence the language in which minority tongues are described. Most accounts and descriptions of the Irish language, for example, are written in English even though the majority of people who study the Irish language are actually in favour of its support and maintenance.

Another important factor is that the themes of linguistic death, decay and pollution have become so commonplace in academic circles that they are almost accepted as natural processes which agree with the proper order of things. This is especially true in the case of Celtic languages. It is often assumed in writings on the subject that the spread of English in Ireland was a choice made freely and willingly by the majority of Ireland's population. This is the theme of Reg Hindley's 1990 book, *The Death of the Irish Language: a qualified obituary*, which has had enormous influence on academics and, perhaps, on government bodies in Ireland. There are still commentators who disagree with Hindley's reading, one of whom, Éamonn Ó Cíosáin, writes:

> The use of the death theme shifts the focus away from any notion

of a language being marginalised and oppressed to a passive idea that the language itself is not fit for survival in a modern society (Ó Cíosáin 1991).

While these words may be considered too strong to describe the position of minority linguistic groups within democratic/liberal states in the modern world, I do not myself believe that they are inappropriate. Marginalisation and oppression can take place at many different levels, and all their effects at all levels can influence how languages are perceived and treated. Richard Krauss puts a similar argument in another way:

> The circumstances which have led to the present language mortality known to us range from outright genocide, social or economic or habitat destruction, displacement, demographic submersion, language suppression, enforced assimilation or assimilatory education to electronic media bombardment, especially television, an incalculably lethal new weapon, which I have called 'cultural nerve gas' (Krauss 1992:8).

The linguistic shift which took place in Ireland can be almost fully explained through the concept of language and power. Until the 17th century the Irish language was used by almost every group and class on the island. The status of Irish changed dramatically however after the Battle of Kinsale in 1601 and it is no exaggeration to say that English speakers, because of their powerful position marginalised the Irish language: at first militarily, then politically, then economically and then socially. By 1800 it was clear that no-one seeking to improve or even maintain his or her social or economic position could do so without the English language (Wall 1969). In the final stages, during the nineteenth century, English was viewed as the natural and essential medium of Irish society, in politics, economics, education and in the media.

The struggle of the native Irish in the 18th and 19th centuries was one for religious and political, rather than linguistic rights, and these religious and political rights were firmly set within an English language context. The perception that it was more effective, and, indeed, more natural to use English than Irish had become the norm to such an extent that Irish nationalists such as Daniel O'Connell and the Young Irelanders used English to promote their political causes, even while the language was still widely spoken. As the English governmental system became more responsive to the demands of marginalised groups in society, the influence of the English language actually increased (Ó Murchú 1971). The more Ireland prospered, the more public service and education systems developed, and the more democratic the state system became, the more the country became anglicised. This occurred in spite of or, it should be argued, because of, considerable concessions to the Catholic Irish, many of whom were still Irish-speaking. English had been accepted as the official language of instruction of St. Patrick's College, Maynooth, the training college for Roman Catholic priests from its foundation in 1795, and the most dramatic fall in the number of Irish-speakers in Ireland came after the remaining Penal Laws had been rescinded with Catholic Emancipation in 1829.

Those areas in which Irish language maintenance did occur were isolated, impoverished, unproductive, very poor - and declining. They had ageing populations, low marriage and birth rates and high rates of emigration - an experience which still causes people to associate the Irish language, and other minority languages, with poverty, filth and backwardness, co-existing with a romantic cult of the Irish speaker as a noble poetic savage (Tovey 1978, CILAR 1975, Ó Donnaile 1994). In this century the decline of the language can be traced. In Ulster alone since 1920 surviving Irish-speaking areas died out in Antrim, Armagh, Tyrone, Derry, Cavan and Monaghan. The process of decline is still in operation today. Even native Irish-speakers can show a preference for English rather than Irish (Ó Donnaile *op cit:* 210, 235). Similar processes concerning dialect can also be observed where speakers of certain dialects demonstrate more favourable attitudes to perceived standard dialects than to their own (Ó Donnaile *op cit:* 241-2).

Ng & Bradac (1993) in their book *Power in Language: Verbal Communication and Social Influence* explain eloquently how certain languages or dialects become dominant:

> The process whereby a particular language or variety becomes dominant is politically complex and often marked by resistance on the part of the dominated party. It involves, among other things, language change which results in the adoption of the dominant language for regular usage. Becoming dominant involves becoming natural, that is, moving from a marked to an unmarked status. When this occurs, we can say that language dominance is routinised in everyday life. (Ng et al 1993:79).

Through time, powerless persons may come to have negative feelings about their own native language or dialect. It is perceived to be at best incorrect and at worst a symbol of inferiority.

One example of these negative feelings towards a minority language can be seen in attitudes towards the decline of Manx. In the 19th century almost all the leaders of Manx society felt that Manx should disappear completely from the face of the earth. English was perceived as being the sole medium for gaining advancement, and Manx as a bar to progress. This attitude can be witnessed in an almost hysterical letter published in the *Manx Advertiser* in 1821, and signed 'yours, a native'. It goes as follows:

> What better is the gibberish called Manx than an uncouth mouthful of course (sic) savage expressions ... abolish the Manx: I would say then, as fast as ye can, ye learned of the country. Judges Lawyers, Clergy, crush it. Allow no one, not even one of your servants or neighbours to speak one word of Manx: and thus, by degrees, annihilate it.

To quote again from Ng & Bradac:

> Thus powerless persons who find themselves using the foreign language may come to have positive feelings about the language even in situations in which their initial feelings were negative.

This might be the case especially when the powerless communicate primarily with those in power (who presumably 'like' the language) and when they perceive themselves as not being coerced into using the language. Gradually the foreign language may come to seem natural and a part of the self (*ibid*: 181).

One of the most interesting features of minority/majority relationships and one which has particular relevance to this discussion is that people become active in their own assimilation to the majority. Corson, using the concept of hegemony first forwarded by Antoin Gramsci, explains how the powerful culture influences and affects the minority in an indirect, invisible and almost subconscious way:

> In developed modern societies, control is exercised in a modern way which gives stability by basing power on wide-ranging consent and agreement (what we might call democracy). This non-coercive force is said to penetrate consciousness itself so that the dominated become accomplices in their own domination ... On a linguistic level we can say that power hegemonies are reinforced from both sides of the power relationship; in their language usages the non-dominant adhere to the linguistic norms created by dominant groups while not recognising that they are being voluntarily coerced (Corson 1993).

If both sides conspire (often unconsciously) in the oppression of the minority, it is possible that even if the majority is favourable and tries to be sensitive to the needs and wishes of the minority, because of the very nature of the power relationship, a linguistic and cultural situation can be created that will damage the minority's culture. Evidence can again be given of cases where minority groups internalise external opinions of themselves and choose only to highlight or encourage those aspects of their own culture which are felt to be acceptable or accessible, or to adapt or 'sanitise' their own culture in such a way as to make it more attractive or less 'threatening' to the more powerful. (It seems that the world's tourist industry is fashioned like this). It is often the case that a group of native Irish speakers will use English to accommodate just one non-Irish speaker.

Language and Social Networks

In spite of the patterns of persistent and continuous oppression outlined above, which can be blatant or subtle, or even subconscious, minority languages still exist and, in the case of Irish, appear to be thriving. Some sociolinguists have studied the conditions which enable minority languages like Irish to have survived at all in spite of continuous oppression.

One useful tool, itself related to the concept of language and power, can help our understanding of this phenomenon. The study of how language functions within social networks can provide some explanation of the continued maintenance of a number of minority languages or dialects in circumstances in which, by any other rational criteria, the dominant linguistic standard would be expected to prevail. Basically it is argued that the survival of a dialect or language reflects the strength, density or self-sufficiency of the social network which sustains it. Such social networks can be based within a wide range of circumstances, embracing working-class urban communities, strongly bonded rural communities and communities linked by religion.

In the close-knit community people have more than one relationship with each other, e.g. one person could be simultaneously a friend, fellow worker, neighbour and relative. In strong community networks, values, attitudes and behaviour are often shared by all the members. Group members are often under pressure to behave in a certain way to be accepted by the community, and there is often hostility to outsiders. In Belfast it is often considered to be dangerous to go into the residential areas of another religious group. This reflects not only the reality of sectarianism, but also the nature of how working-class social networks function in urban societies throughout the world. The close-knit urban network has a conception of the street or neighbourhood as an extension of the home (Freid 1971). What used to be called 'corner boys' actually mark the territory of the social network (Milroy 1980).

Hostility is not confined to outsiders: people who transgress the norms of the group can be shunned, ridiculed and excluded from the network. This power of the network over its members can stifle some but can also provide support, protection and security. Social sanctions can also be applied to linguistic behaviour. Kenneth MacKinnon (1977) cites an example of a woman in a Gaeltacht in Scotland who was mocked as a snob because she spoke English to her children.

The literature of sociolinguistics gives many examples of minority dialects or languages being strongest in close-knit communities: farmers in Austria, New York gang culture, rural and urban groups in Norway. One example relevant to the Irish language in Northern Ireland can be seen in the experience of members of the Shaw's Road Gaeltacht community in West Belfast, a community which is about 30 years old. In her book *Our Own Language - an Irish Initiative* Dr Gabrielle Maguire writes that the people who moved to the Shaw's Road Gaeltacht understood that they would have to gaelicise as many speech events and situations as possible and that they would have to create strong Irish-speaking social networks to defend the use of Irish. She writes:

> The introduction and establishment of Irish in various sociolinguistic domains was clearly being achieved by the Shaw's Road parents. From the beginning, the home and later the school represented the strongholds in the work of rearing Irish-speaking children ... the cluster of eleven houses on Shaw's Road, with their nursery and primary school situated just beyond their back gardens, comprised a closely-knit community in a physical as well as a social sense. Indeed, many of the families were related to each other so that some of the children live next door to their cousins (Maguire, 1991:81).

If strong and dense social networks aid the maintenance of minority languages or dialects, they will be correspondingly threatened by any weakening of the density, power or control of the network. At the same time, no minority networks are free from the influence of broader society. Nor is any community totally immune from the effects of developments and changes in the state, especially when that community seeks state support and protection.

Some Implications of Majority Support

Another feature of minority language maintenance involves resistance to linguistic shift or cultural pressure. At a certain point in the marginalisation of minority language groups, when speakers of a language stop speaking it, or when the number of minority speakers becomes dangerously low, we almost always find individuals and groups concerned with revival and maintenance movements. Language groups of both natives and learners appear - demanding political and civil rights for their language communities.

It is this process of agitating for - and often gaining - concessions from centralised governments and bodies that sits at the core of the question posed at the beginning of this paper: 'Can minorities cope with a favourable majority?'

Most western states subscribe to the democratic principles of equity, justice and tolerance. Many of them, however continue to struggle with an historic legacy of hostility to minorities rooted in early attempts to create unified, homogenous states. Linguistic minorities in western cultures demand, struggle for and sometimes are given certain rights within the state such as education and access to the media. But how much actual power is a centralised state prepared - or able - to give to the minority? Too much may undermine the integrity of the state, too little will leave it open to accusations of being undemocratic and oppressive.

Modern democratic states instinctively tend to give their minorities minimum power (Williams 1978). The support given is usually weighed by state-inspired conditions which reflect the values of the state rather than those of the minority.

Government control features highly in the case of expenditure on the Irish language in Northern Ireland. Groups which receive funding or sponsorship must act responsibly (in the view of the donor), projects should attract people who are not in the minority group, be accessible to majority group members, and be economically viable. In this way the power of the minority is controlled and monitored. Those groups which do not appear to conform with state policy on the promotion of minority culture are less likely to receive help. Government ideology is the net beneficiary in such a situation, and it is not uncommon for groups to change structure, membership, outlook and even aims for the sake of financial aid.

That the above analysis is more than simply a conspiracy theory may be illustrated from the Welsh situation. The survival of the Welsh language was originally based on dense rural communities underpinned by the strong institutional support of the nonconformist churches. These developed in the 19th century into close-knit mining communities which themselves greatly supported the maintenance of the language. Although Welsh was in quite a strong position, because Welsh-speaking people had no control over their own economic conditions, the decline of the coal industry over thirty years ago had enormous implications for Welsh. Social networks broke up and were diluted by the movement of people and industry (Thomas 1987). Economic forces operating primarily through the medium of English became increasingly important. The Welsh language movement agitated so successfully for formal and legal recognition of the language that Welsh is often seen as being the model of a minority language success story. Some academics in Wales, however, are reluctant to agree.

Williams, writing as long ago as twenty years, argues that in spite of successes in education, politics, the media and many other aspects of life, Welsh speakers were still oppressed by English-speaking forces. He describes Welsh society as two separate, almost identical systems existing side by side - the only difference between them is a language difference. The

Welsh language social system almost exactly mirrors the English language system: in both groups, control and evaluation of cultural capital is exercised by academics who control cultural reproduction (something that has led to an impoverishment of the language), and by the business class (who operate a system based entirely on the English-language world). Despite advances in the institutional support for Welsh, Williams feels that Welsh continues to be in danger. He argues that people are blind to the other baggage that state support brings with it, and that Welsh activists and academics focused their analysis of the situation and their demands on the political and symbolic levels rather than achieving real autonomy. He recommends that minority activists redefine the language struggle in terms of the economic framework rather than that of the symbolic.

> It is the focusing of such a struggle on the political or the superstructure rather than the economic or the infrastructure which constitutes the ideological basis of the context in which language tends to be discussed. As such it is a situation which by focusing on the promise to a solution to the language problem at the political level inspires minority speakers to fight for access within a political sphere divorced from their own economic condition, i.e. they aspire to a political life based on their own exploitation. The 'taken for granted' nature of the role of the dominant language within the economic sphere facilitates this process while also underlining its role as a feature of the hegemonic order which creates the 'taken for granted'.

Because in the Welsh situation the Welsh-speaking social structure almost exactly mirrors that of English speakers, where Welsh people have certain linguistic rights under an English-language economic system which promotes associated values, Williams argues that there have been successive generations of people who speak Welsh but who think and act as if they were English.

This description of the Welsh situation has resonances for our own position here in Northern Ireland, where people who are similar in many ways are divided not on linguistic but on religious lines. Because attention is focused on religion or symbolic issues (important as they are) rather than class or economic background, other forms of imbalance and injustice can be perpetuated in society. Minority oppression (except in religious forms) and economic exploitation can be neglected.

Conclusion

I have argued that the state works on many levels from outright oppression and conscious domination to an unconscious 'taken-for-granted' attitude which is often shared with the minority. Both groups, as I have said, conspire in this. However, the dominance of the state or of the majority can be affected by a number of factors: the strength and social cohesion of minority groups, the enthusiasm and awareness of the minority, the degree of difference between the two groups, the distance between majority and minority groups and the relative power and control exercised by both in every domain of life.

People in minority groups often aspire to rights on a political or symbolic level but not in terms of actual power or in terms of control of their own economy. Often, it is true, this will be the only way of gaining support. In other words they often aspire to rights and recognition within a system which is, consciously or subconsciously, intentionally or unintentionally, geared towards their own oppression or, at the very least, the dilution of their own culture. However, the minority group views each minor concession as a great victory.

In addressing this discussion to an Irish-speaking minority (and I believe this discussion also has relevance for other minorities), I would suggest that the achievement of even hard-won rights can be a mixed blessing. It must be remembered that support, funding and opportunity have a price. The American Dream of democracy, free speech and free market opportunities seemed to offer everything and seemed to ask for nothing in return but hard work and commitment. However, the price most immigrant groups paid for the privilege of participating in the new value system and of availing of the new opportunities was the loss of their cultures.

To members of the majority who may feel that they have been unfairly treated in this article I would like to say that such a response itself reflects the very nature of our relationship. No criticism of one particular government or state or system or even a certain group of individuals was intended. The processes I have described here can be seen all over the world in many different situations. But I would ask the majority to be aware of their influence.

Many people in our society who would regard themselves as tolerant will defend the right of people to speak Irish, but are insulted if the language is spoken in front of them. This seems to come from a perception that it is normal and acceptable to speak English in Ireland but it can be bad-mannered, insensitive or even sometimes politically subversive to speak Irish or use the language publicly. It is often argued that, as virtually everyone can speak English in Northern Ireland, the English language will not present a problem. To quote again from the Government statement mentioned at the beginning of this article 'Virtually everyone who uses Irish in Northern Ireland will have English as a first language and will suffer no practical inconvenience from using English'. That is an excellent example of the point I am making. In situations of language contact powerful groups do not usually become bi-lingual. It is the powerless who are forced to learn and then use the dominant language - South Americans learned Spanish, Rwandan peoples learned French and the Celts learned English. Some of the original languages were lost, and many of those which survived are in danger of extinction.

I am well aware that my argument presents a dilemma for the minority. Without majority support or help from the powerful the minority group might not survive, but what are the consequences of that support and help? I hope this article will encourage more openness and a different kind of debate than that which is commonly held both within and outside the

Irish language community. In the period of political change which approaches the language question will become increasingly significant and it will be important for all groups to be aware of the implications of decisions.

The Irish language package *Ciste Cúrsaí Reatha* (De Fréine 1985), cites an observation by Seán Philpott Ó Corráin (1755-1817) on democratic freedom 'The condition upon which God hath given liberty to man is eternal vigilance': to use Ó Corráin's own native tongue: 'Ní saoirse go síorfhaire'.

References

CILAR 1975
Committee on Irish Language Attitudes Research Report, Dublin, The Stationery Office.

Corson 1991
D Corson, 'Language power and minority schooling', *Language and Education*, 5. (4). 231-253

De Fréine 1978
Seán de Fréine, *The Great Silence*. Dublin & Cork: Mercier Press.

Freid 1973
M Freid, *The World of the Urban Working Class*. Cambridge, Mass.: Harvard University Press.

Hindley 1990
R Hindley, *The Death of the Irish Language: a qualified obituary*. London: Routledge.

Krauss 1992
M Krauss, 'The worlds' languages in crisis', *Language*, 68(1), 4-10.

Maguire 1991
Gabrielle Maguire, *Our Own Language - An Irish Initiative*. Clevedon: Multilingual Matters Ltd.

MacKinnon 1977
Kenneth MacKinnon, *Language Education and Social Processes in a Gaeltacht Community*. London: Routledge & Kegan Paul Ltd.

MacKinnon 1991
Kenneth MacKinnon, 'The Gaelic Speech Community', S. Alladina & V. Edwards (ed.) Multilingualism in the British Isles: *The Older Mother Tongues and Europe*, 49-67. London: Longman.

Milroy 1980
L Milroy, *Language and Social Networks*. Oxford: Blackwell.

Ng & Bradach 1993
S H Ng & J J Bradach, *Power in Language: Verbal Communication and Social Influence*. London: Sage Publications.

Ó Cíosáin 1991
Éamonn Ó Cíosáin, *Buried Alive: A Reply to the Death of the Irish Language*. Baile Átha Cliath: Dáil Uí Chadhain.

Ó Donnaile 1994
Antaine Ó Donnaile, *Staidéar Sochtheangeolaíoch ar Cheantar Ghaoth Dobhair*. (PhD Thesis) University of Ulster.

Ó Murchú 1970
Máirtín Ó Murchú, *Urlabhra agus Pobal*. Comhairle na Gaeilge, Páipéar Ócáidiúil Uimhir I. Baile Átha Cliath: Oifig an tSoláthair.

Ó Riagáin 1992
Pádraig Ó Riagáin, *Language Maintenance and Language Shift as Strategies of Social Reproduction: Irish in the Corca Dhuibhne Gaeltacht 1926-1986*. Baile Átha Cliath: ITÉ.

Thomas 1986
B Thomas, 'Accounting for language maintenance and shift: socio-historical evidence from a mining community in Wales', G. Mac Eoin, A. Ahlqvist & D. Ó hAodha (ed.), *Third International Paper on Minority Languages: Celtic Papers*. Clevedon, Philadelphia: Multilingual Matters Ltd.

Tovey 1978
Hilary Tovey, *Language Policy and Socioeconomic Development in Ireland*, ITÉ Páipéar Ócáide 4. Baile Átha Cliath: ITÉ.

Wall 1969
Maureen Wall, 'The Decline of the Irish Language', B. Ó Cuív (ed.), *A View of the Irish Language*, 81-90. Dublin: Stationery office.

Williams 1982
G Williams, 'Language maintenance and language shift in Wales', P. Ó Riagáin (ed.), *Taighde Sochtheangeolaíochta agus Teangeolaíochta sa Ghaeltacht: Riachtanais an Lae Inniu*, 47-56. Baile Átha Cliath: ITÉ.

Notes on contributers

Liam Andrews is a native of Belfast. He studied Celtic Languages at Queen's University, Belfast, and Education at the University College of Wales, Aberystwyth. He speaks Irish and Welsh fluently. He is a member of the Shaw's Road Irish-language community in west Belfast and is a former chairman of the Management Committees of *Bunscoil Phobal Feirste* and *Meánscoil Feirste*. His research on the Irish language in Northern Ireland has been supported by a Teacher Fellowship at the University of Ulster in 1987 and an EC research grant in 1989. In 1993 he published a major report on the Irish language and the training of teachers in Northern Ireland. Currently he is completing a history of the treatment of the language in Northern Ireland.

Gordon McCoy hails from Saintfield and is a past pupil of Down High School, Downpatrick. After working for seven years in the civil service he studied for a degree in Celtic and Social Anthropology at Queen's University, Belfast. Afterwards he remained at the university to examine Protestant learners of Irish for a doctoral thesis in the Department of Social Anthropology. He is currently employed as a cross-community officer with the ULTACH Trust.

Aodán Mac Póilin was born in Belfast, and educated by the Christian Brothers and at the University of Ulster. Worked as a teacher and is currently director of ULTACH Trust. Involved in the Irish language movement since 1971, and is a former chairman of the first Irish-medium school in Northern Ireland. Irish-language editor of the literary journal *Krino*. Author of two pamphlets on broadcasting and was co-editor of *The Selected Poems of Padraic Fiacc*, 1994, and *Styles of Belonging: The Cultural Identity of Ulster*, 1991.

Ian Malcolm: from what he describes as the liberal unionist tradition, Ian Malcolm is a journalist with specific interests in political development and the Irish language. He works as a sub-editor with the *News Letter* in Belfast, but writes regularly for a wide range of Irish language publications, as well as contributing to both *Raidió na Gaeltachta* and *Teilifís na Gaeilge*.

Antaine Ó Donnaile is a native of Armagh and past pupil of the Christian Brothers Grammar School there. After finishing a degree in Irish Studies at the University of Ulster at Coleraine he went on to complete his doctoral thesis - a sociolinguistic study of the Gaoth Dobhair area - *Staidéar Sochtheangeolaíoch ar Cheantar Ghaoth Dobhair, Co. Dhún na nGall* (1994). Antaine is also a keen Irish language dramatist and has written, directed and acted in many plays. He is an adjudicator with *An Comhlachas Náisiúnta Drámaíochta*. He has been working for the past two years as a producer and presenter with the BBC's Irish language unit.

Camille O'Reilly is an American academic who grew up in Los Angeles. She studied for her primary degree at the University of California, Berkeley, and has an MA and a PhD in Social Anthropology from Queen's University Belfast. Her doctorate, *Fíor-Ghaeil: The Politics of the Irish Language in West Belfast*, is to be published soon by Macmillan. At present, she is lecturing in Social Anthropology in Richmond, the American International University in London. She learned Irish when doing her research and maintains a strong interest in the language.

**16242 -
000475**